PREACHING CHRISTIAN DOCTRINE

To: Stacy Johnson,
a great theologian and a
great teacher —

From your colleague
in ministry and
theological education —

William J Carl III

PREACHING CHRISTIAN DOCTRINE

WILLIAM J. CARL III

FORTRESS PRESS   PHILADELPHIA

Library of Congress Cataloging in Publication Data

Carl, William J.
    Preaching Christian doctrine.

    1. Preaching. I. Title.
    BV4211.2.C27   1984   251   83-48923
    ISBN 0-8006-1788-6

K116B84   Printed in the United States of America   1–1788

To My Father

CONTENTS

PREFACE

This book arises out of a love of preaching and a deep interest in doctrine. In my own struggle to do a better job of the former and to know more of the latter, I have sought to order my thinking about both. Perhaps this systematic approach to doctrinal preaching will help others in the church. That is my hope.

Although this book is written in the form of a text with the seminary classroom in mind, my real audience is the pastor. Thus, the book points beyond the rarified air of academia to the theological world of the parish. To assure that, I waited to write the book until after my sabbatic leave spent as a one-year full-time interim pastor of River Road Presbyterian Church in Richmond, Virginia. To that congregation I want to offer appreciation for listening to my own doctrinal sermons, for demanding substance in preaching, and for helping me see that Christians today want to be taught the doctrines of the faith from the pulpit.

Much of the material presented in this book has been tested in lectures and workshops at Princeton, Pittsburgh, McCormick, Columbia, Wartburg, and Union (Virginia) seminaries, as well as at the Luther Academy of the Rockies in Colorado. Many students and pastors have helped sharpen my thinking on this subject.

I want to thank my homiletics professors, George Arthur Buttrick and David G. Buttrick, both of whom inspired my continued interest in preaching. Thanks also to colleagues at Union Seminary in Virginia, whose conversations made this a better manuscript: Douglas F. Ottati, D. Cameron Murchison, John Leith, Charles Swezey, Donald Dawe, William V. Arnold, F. Wellford Hobbie, and Elizabeth Achtemeier. I want to thank John Hollar

1

of Fortress Press for his continued interest in this book. Without Sally Hicks the manuscript would never have made it to the publisher. Without the support of my wife, Jane, and sons, Jeremy and David, I would never have finished the book.

My earliest memories of sound doctrinal preaching are still clear in my mind. I can still hear my father holding forth with solid theological teaching and a doctrinal sustenance that speaks to the human soul. To that committed preacher of the Word, I dedicate this book.

William J. Carl, III
Union Theological Seminary, Richmond
August 1983

ONE

Preaching
and Theology

Preaching Christian doctrine has always been a priority in the church. Major theologians, such as Thomas Aquinas, John Calvin, Martin Luther, Paul Tillich, and others, are known not only for their systems of thought but for their ability to bring theology to life in the Sunday sermon. They preached doctrine because they knew that an ignorant laity leads to an impotent church, and that clergy and laity need sound doctrine, preached boldly and simply, in order to live and grow in the Christian faith.

This assertion is more than an academic plea for intellectual stimulation. It recognizes that believers suffer from a theological identity crisis, and that it is the church's role to help people discover who they are as Christians. Many church members today do not know what they believe. "All religions are alike," they will say. "It doesn't matter what you believe as long as you believe something."

This theological identity crisis is the church's most serious problem, for it affects all other areas of the church's life. When people do not know what they believe, they cannot be expected to worship, nurture, or go into the world ministering and acting in Christ's name. Since theology is to discipleship as botany is to gardening, an understanding of what one is doing will help clarify the difference between pruning and weeding.[1] Doctrine and experience always have been inextricably bound together. Practice without doctrine is often misguided. Action without belief can go astray.

Increasing secular pluralism and shrinking attendance in adult Sunday-school classes have contributed to this theological identity problem. Little wonder that believers find it hard to know

3

what to believe. They live in a secular world. Their questions are, for the most part, not religious questions or, at least, they are not framed that way. Most Christians join the church as youngsters, and any serious learning in the faith seems to stop at that point. They go through their entire lives with only a tacit knowledge of Christian beliefs and values, often a knowledge they have received and a faith they have inherited from their parents or other significant persons in their lives. Perhaps some attend adult Sunday-school classes where one of two activities often occurs. Either they hear someone read a lesson on a Bible passage or they discuss a specific social issue, sharing and debating opinions that are uninformed by Christian doctrine.

Another reason for the identity crisis has been the pervasive lack of able doctrinal preaching in the American church for most of this century. The transformation from exegetical and theological preaching to a more topical, psychotherapeutic kind of preaching may be marked by Harry Emerson Fosdick's 1928 *Harpers* article, "What Is the Matter with Preaching?" People do not come to church with a burning interest in what happened to the Jebusites, Fosdick said, but with their own questions and problems. Although Fosdick was more theologically astute and responsible than many who have followed his "problem-solution approach," he was also quite neohumanistic in his answers to people's problems. The gospel was often accompanied by great art, music, and the highest in cultural representation as the solution to various problems. Topical preaching began to overtake exegetical and theological preaching, except in some Lutheran and Presbyterian circles. Certainly topical preaching seemed more interesting and relevant to people's lives.

I do not mean to imply that before 1928 people were growing in the faith more than after 1928. Fosdick was probably right: in the nineteenth and early twentieth centuries, many people were going to church only to hear theological lectures or exegetical papers. They were either bored or did not understand, since doctrine that is not seen in the context of human life is neither comprehensible nor helpful.

Reacting to this aridity, many American preachers introduced sermons on "How to Have a Happy Family," "How to Feel Good About Yourself," and other such topics. "All the evidence goes to show that a great deal of Protestant preaching for a generation past has been on marginal things," wrote British clergyman W. E. Sangster in 1953.[2] It is a safe bet that his analysis would not have changed much after thirty years. The church today, just as the early church and the church of the Reformation and the two Great Awakenings, needs clear and sound preaching on the doctrines of the faith.

Definitions

What is doctrinal preaching? Let us begin with some definitions. I want to argue first that all preaching, to be authentic Christian preaching, is or at least should be grounded in Scripture. That is to say, all Christian preaching is or should be either explicitly or implicitly informed by the Bible.

At the same time, all Christian preaching is doctrinal. This latter statement is entirely descriptive, whereas the former is both descriptive and prescriptive. The preacher who delivers a sermon in the pulpit is presenting doctrine. He or she may not be aware of it, but that is what is happening. The sermon may be heresy or it may be humanism, but it is always doctrine of some kind. Doctrine is presented in the sermon's illustrative material (sometimes vividly) and through various ways that the preacher interprets Christian tradition (Scripture, creeds, and the like) and contemporary experience. The congregation may or may not be able to name the specific doctrine or doctrines being presented. But if they hear and understand what is being said, they are being shaped and molded in their views of God and the Christian life.

The way the congregation hears the message is often governed by at least two presuppositions or hidden agendas. One presupposition that should be taken into account is what the preacher is trying to do theologically with his or her sermons. What is happening in this sermon? What am I trying to do here? Is this sermon functioning as a saving word of grace? Is it a judging word? These are good questions to ask. For Martin Luther, the sermon would have been a justifying word; for John Calvin, a saving word with an instructional sense and an emphasis on the law, particularly its third use, where the saints grow in the faith in response to grace. For John Wesley, it would have been a sanctifying word. What am I trying to do here? Teach? Inspire? How am I trying to do this theologically?

The other presupposition or hidden agenda is one the congregation brings. People go to church with various expectations about what should happen in a sermon. "I want to be invited to have a personal relationship with Jesus Christ." "I want to be comforted in the midst of my sorrow." "I want to be challenged to act in the community." "I want new insight." Many church members do not consciously think about their presuppositions, but if asked they could verbalize them. Most people have only one presupposition, but not the same one. This plethora of presuppositions may be a blessing or a curse for the preacher. We will deal with reasons for these many presuppositions in a subsequent chapter. For now it is sufficient to note that the people who come to our churches and sit in our pews are at various stages in the Christian pilgrimage. They come implicitly asking doctrinal questions, and they expect answers.

Part of our responsibility as preachers is to identify the doctrinal hermeneutic that governs our own preaching. Some of us have a high Christology, like the Gospel of John or the epistle to the Hebrews, which tends to appear in every sermon and which dictates the way we present a biblical text or doctrine. Others of us fall on one side or the other of the world view presented in the Gospel of John. We see creation as good, or we deny the world and retreat from it. For still others, the doctrinal hermeneutic may be a repeated emphasis on sin and the cross. Whatever the case, we preachers need to identify the doctrine (and there usually is one) that colors our preaching, that gives it not only content but ethos. Moreover, we should try as much as possible to identify the doctrines or at least the questions that lurk in the congregation and in the culture.

So all Christian preaching is doctrinal and is or should be biblical. The confusion over these terms usually arises when we use them separately, as if they described two distinct forms of preaching. They do not.

When we use these terms separately, we are usually talking about the starting place for preparing a sermon. Do you start with a text or with a doctrine? When people say they start with a text, they often go on to say that they are doing biblical preaching, whether they stick with that text or not. Others, starting with a doctrine, say they are doing doctrinal preaching, even though they may devote most of their sermon to an exposition of the text.

I believe there are only two types of preaching: textual and topical. Therefore, the preacher either begins with a text and lays it open for a congregation, or begins with a topic, that is, a doctrine explicitly chosen for the occasion or chosen in response to some question or statement that has been raised in the congregation or the culture. The topical starting point could also be a social issue that the preacher has decided to address as an informed interpreter of the Word. In any case, the responsible preacher does not merely present his or her own views regarding a particular doctrine or social issue, but does extensive work in the Bible and in the theological tradition on the topic in question. This usually involves more extensive study than a textual sermon, and thus should probably not be attempted every week.

In the course of research, one or possibly two texts will emerge as a ground for the sermon on the particular doctrine or issue in question. These texts are not selected so that the preacher can "baptize" an idea that has previously been thought through. No matter how tempting such a process may be, it should be resisted, for it runs the risk of preaching a doctrinal sermon that is not biblically informed.

The situation in a particular parish or congregation may dictate the preacher's choice of texts. For example, a preacher may see the need to present a sermon on law and gospel or faith and works. If the preacher chooses Pauline texts on these themes, the doctrinal sermon that emerges will offer a different message from one using Matthew or James as the starting point. This is more than a matter of doctrinal diversity in the New Testament. It involves also the pastor's relationship to a congregation and his or her reading of the culture. The pastor's own theological tradition will influence this choice as well. For example, Lutherans might look to Paul for law/gospel, faith/works emphases, whereas those within the Calvinist and Thomistic traditions might turn instead to Matthew and James. Whatever the case, biblical texts need to be examined and taken seriously in the formation of a doctrinal sermon.

For many, the texts are already selected by a lectionary. Many find this *lectio selecta* approach highly liberating and only diverge from it when they have a specific topic (doctrine or social issue) that needs to be addressed—one that is not dealt with specifically in the Sunday lesson. Those following a *lectio continua* approach—going pericope by pericope through a book of the Bible—also begin with a text. Beginning with a text does not mean that you will stay with it. Many preachers begin with a text but soon leave it behind. Conversely, responsible preachers open the text for the congregation. This is usually called expository preaching. Structurally, the sermon may proceed verse by verse through the text, or it may find the text opening into two to four natural points. Expository preaching may also move around in the text with a dialogical approach, questioning and listening to the text.

In the course of exegetical work, one finds that even with a narrative passage, certain doctrines begin to emerge. It is possible, then, that what began Monday morning as an expository sermon on a specific text may find itself in the pulpit Sunday morning as a full-blown doctrinal sermon. Thus, it appears that there is a great deal of overlap between the terms "doctrinal" and "biblical" in Christian preaching.

The following diagram demonstrates the process of Christian preaching. Assuming that the primary purpose of preaching is to present the good news of Jesus Christ, we begin with the biblical witness to that fact and its doctrinal clarification. This is the ground of all preaching. With texts and topics as starting points, we then move through the process of constructing either an expository or a doctrinal sermon. *Doctrinal preaching, then, is Christian preaching grounded in the biblical witness to Jesus*

Christ; it starts with text, doctrine, or cultural question, but tends to focus on one or more Christian doctrines regardless of its starting point.

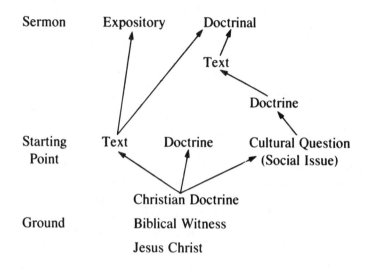

Purpose and Plan

This book aims to help the preacher proclaim Christian doctrine cogently and effectively. Just as systematic theology attempts to organize and present theology in an orderly manner, so this book attempts to organize and present homiletics in a systematic manner. We begin with an analysis of the audience and the problems of using theological language in the pulpit (chapter 2) as the preacher presents doctrine to a socially fragmented and theologically diverse group of hearers. From here we move systematically through the three starting points for a doctrinal sermon: text, doctrine, and question or statement arising in church and culture (chapters 3, 4, and 5). Thus from exegetical theology we move to polemics, catechesis, apologetics, pastoral care, ethics, and evangelism. Such movement represents a conscious attempt to keep doctrinal preaching grounded in Scripture and to progress from a lesser to a greater degree of difficulty.

The simplest way to assure that doctrinal preaching remains

grounded in Scripture is to begin with Scripture. Through the centuries Christian preaching has often begun with the biblical text. But it has not always mined the text for its doctrinal richness. Chapter 3 thus examines ways of determining biblical doctrine by exploring the fruits and faults of the biblical theology movement and the impact of form and redaction criticism on doctrinal preaching.

Catechetical and polemical preaching are not new to the church. Catechumens were often nurtured in the faith through preaching and instruction concerning the sacraments and creeds. Polemics more than apologetics remains within the arena of the church, the community of faith, and tends to concentrate on in-house questions. While polemics, like apologetics, has to do with correct thinking about the faith (orthodoxy), its focus is more on exposing and rooting out incorrect thinking (heterodoxy) within the faith. It is unfortunate that the word "heresy" is such a red flag in our time, recalling the heresy hunts and trials that used to occur, but seldom do in the church today. In times like ours, when people believe in "doing their own thing" and certainly "thinking their own thing" (if, in fact, some are thinking at all about religion), the mode of theological discourse called polemics is certainly in order. Doctrinal preaching, which includes polemics, is not intended to raise a homiletical lynch mob, but to help Christians understand more clearly who they are.

Certainly this has been the primary role of polemics throughout Christian history. Examples of this in the New Testament can be found in the book of Acts and in Paul's letters—particularly Romans, 1 Corinthians, and Galatians. Look also at Irenaeus (*Against Heresies*), Tertullian, Augustine (against the Donatists and Pelagians), Thomas Aquinas (with his *Summa Theologica* and the *Compendium Theologiae*), Luther, Calvin, and Jonathan Edwards.

The benefits of this kind of preaching are immediately obvious. Such doctrines as baptism, the Holy Spirit, the meaning of heaven and hell, and the like are so wide and varied, and create so much consternation for the individual believer and so much dissension among the churches, that clear, precise polemical preaching is sorely needed today. Chapter 4 takes up this issue in more detail.

Chapter 5 looks at doctrinal preaching that begins with the culture, that is, from the point of view of apologetics. Apologetics is that mode of theological discourse that rightly belongs in the academy, for it examines the truth of the Christian faith when held up to the light of human reason. Apologetics seeks to defend the Christian faith in the arena of the world, often finding itself employing the world's categories for argument. The audience, therefore, is necessarily those outside the faith, but not exclusively so. Apologetics and evangelism have this in common. Sometimes the two merge, as in Acts 2, when the Jews ask about the behavior of the Christians who were filled with the Holy Spirit on Pentecost. Peter uses the occasion to clarify who the Christians are as a people distinct from the Jews (apologetics) and to tell them about Christ, while also calling on them to repent (evangelism). Often evangelism involves at least implicit apologetics.

Acts 2 is one example of apologetics in theology and preaching. Another possible text is Acts 17:16–34. This Lukan construction of Paul at Athens is an example of a carefully crafted rhetorical utterance designed not only to distinguish and defend the Christian faith but to persuade the hearers to change their point of view. Here Paul addresses the Epicurean and Stoic philosophers in a form of doctrinal preaching that is both apologetic and evangelistic. At least two were convinced: Dionysius the Areopagite and a woman called Damaris. In Acts 26, Paul defends Christianity apologetically and evangelistically (see vv. 28–29).

The tradition of apologetics can be seen throughout the history of theological discourse. From Justin Martyr, with his attacks on Greco-Roman paganism and apostasy from Judaism; to Origen, with his *On First Principles,* for those outside the faith; to Augustine, taking on the Manicheans; to Aquinas, with his *Summa Contra Gentiles;* to Friedrich Schleiermacher, with his *On Religion: Speeches to its Cultured Despisers;* to Søren Kierkegaard; and, finally, to the preaching and writings of Reinhold Niebuhr and Paul Tillich—we find a rich tradition of theologians who show what is distinctive about the Christian faith. Apologetics in doctrinal preaching has been used to help inform the Christian community about its own beliefs as distinguished from the beliefs of the rest of the world. It has drawn lines and given reasons for beliefs which have long been accepted tacitly. Statements like "All religions are alike" or "It doesn't matter what you believe" are perfect starting points for apologetic preaching.

In addition to exegetical theology, polemics, and apologetics, doctrinal preaching should also be informed by ethics. Traditionally, ethics as a discipline would be in the category of philosophical theology, since it relates to what is distinctively human and seeks to organize knowledge concerning "the whole human culture, not morality alone."[3] For our purposes, however, we will talk of it also in the context of practical theology (or the practical side of dogmatic theology), since doctrinal preaching will be more concerned with the moral questions of the believer than with philosophical debates in the field of ethics.[4] If in apologetics and polemics the preacher is concerned with helping the believer understand what to believe, in ethics the preacher is concerned with helping the believer understand what to do. It happens again and again in the Bible; theology leads to ethics, indicative to imperative, belief to action. Consider Paul's arrangement in his letter to the Romans. Chapters 1—11 spell out the theology; chapter 12 begins the ethical instruction. The history of doctrine is a record of this pattern. Dogma leads to praxis. There are those today who move intentionally to this kind of praxis-theology quite early. I am thinking particularly of liberation theologians. But in traditional Western theologies, dogma usually precedes ethics; belief usually precedes action.

Responsible doctrinal preaching not only examines the truth of beliefs and the reasons for these beliefs in the Christian life, it also focuses on moral questions that plague the contemporary believer. Without this moral dimension to doctrinal preaching, the Christian pulpit cannot effectively bring the gospel to bear on people's individual lives and corporately influence or transform culture.

I have argued that one of the most serious problems confronting the church today is the theological identity crisis experienced by the Christian believer. The solution to this problem is twofold:

(1) a sound and critical adult Christian education program; and (2) responsible doctrinal preaching that will not only present the basic truth of Jesus Christ but clarify how the believer shall live under Christ's lordship.

For Reflection

1. What is your theology of preaching? How does it operate in your interpretation of texts and in your presentation of the gospel? In order to be specific, examine various sermons you have preached.

2. What is the theology of preaching that seemed to be present in congregations to which you have belonged or served? Identify how that theology became clear in the comments or questions of church members.

3. Identify in today's church mistaken ideas about the following themes: (a) faith and works; (b) sin and salvation; (c) the incarnation of Jesus Christ; (d) the nature and purpose of the church; (e) good and evil; (f) the work of the Holy Spirit; (g) Christianity and culture; (h) free will; (i) eschatology; and (j) prayer.

Further Reading on This Subject

Baker, Eric. *Preaching Theology*. London: Epworth Press, 1954.

Duke, Robert W. *The Sermon as God's Word: Theologies for Preaching*. Nashville: Abingdon Press, 1980: 97–112.

Ebeling, Gerhard. *Theology and Proclamation: Dialogue with Bultmann*. Philadelphia: Fortress Press, 1966: 13–21.

Lischer, Richard. *A Theology of Preaching*. Nashville: Abingdon Press, 1981: 13–29.

Ott, Heinrich. *Theology and Preaching*. Philadelphia: Westminster Press, 1965: 17–28.

Pitt-Watson, Ian. *Preaching: A Kind of Folly*. Philadelphia: Westminster Press, 1976: 1–35.

Sangster, W. E. *Doctrinal Preaching: Its Neglect and Recovery*. Birmingham, England: Berean Press, 1953: 3–13.

Stuempfle, Herman G., Jr. *Preaching Law and Gospel*. Philadelphia: Fortress Press, 1978: 11–19.

Wedel, Theodore O. *The Pulpit Rediscovers Theology*. New York: Seabury Press, 1956: 3–31.

TWO

Theological
Language in the Pulpit

Responsible doctrinal preaching has always taken seriously the problem of theological language. The New Testament writers themselves offer the best evidence of this fact. The Christ event burst upon the scene in new language created by the evangelists and the writers of the epistles. New life was breathed into already existing terms. The world was renamed in the light of Christ's life, death, and resurrection, never to be the same again. Terms like "justification" and "adoption" took on new meaning as they spread across the Mediterranean world. There was a new excitement generated by this language, an excitement that changed the face of the world.

Understanding the Audience

The first step in the process of correctly appropriating and preaching theology is to know the audience one is addressing. Reginald Fuller makes this clear when he provides example after example of the various approaches to Christology that existed in the New Testament churches.[1] As the biblical writers sought to communicate the gospel effectively to Palestinian Jews, Hellenistic Jews, and Hellenistic Gentiles, they employed images and terms for Christ that would not only be comprehensible to their hearers but would bring them to their knees by touching the emotions and moving the will.

Who is the audience in today's church? What are their interests, their hurts, their attitudes toward religion? What question or questions do they bring? Different theologians respond to these queries in different ways. John Calvin no doubt believed that the question the parishioner brought to church on Sunday was, What

15

can we learn about God and ourselves and how can we glorify him?

Karl Barth believed that the people in the pew were asking humbly and sincerely, Is it true about God? Is there a meaning, a goal, a God? He believed that people were interested in the preacher answering the question about God more than any other question. Most preachers, according to Barth, beat around the bush, entertain, put people off. We should not, he believed, be fooled by a blasé exterior.[2] Behind it is a deep longing to know and meet Christ, not only to hear "yes" in answer to questions, but to confront God.

Paul Tillich believed that people were asking questions about the nature of being in relation to their own lives. Questions about life and death; questions about grief, anxiety, and abandonment. Whereas pastoral counselors deal with problems of psychological anxiety, preachers deal with questions of ontological anxiety. Unlike Barth, Tillich did not always begin with the biblical text. Instead, he often began with these congregational and cultural questions.

Schubert Ogden would say that the parishioners' question is, How can we believe in God and live authentically without a sacrifice in intellect? This is the question of our technological and scientific age. It is the question of the post-Constantinian, post-Christian era.

The question that nineteenth-century liberal theology saw the people in the pew asking was, What can I do to save the world? The liberal theology of Albrecht Ritschl and Adolf von Harnack spoke of humanity's hope, forgetting that in humanity alone there is no hope. Nineteenth-century liberal theology thought it could see progress, and thus preached its own thoughts, convinced that the believer was asking how he or she could participate in the progress of humankind. According to both Barth and Niebuhr, as well as others in the so-called neo-orthodox movement, this was a faulty and misguided question. Niebuhr, for example, believed that far from being the answer, Christ becomes the problem. The parishioners' question, as he saw it, was, What shall I do, then, with this Jesus who is called the Christ? For Niebuhr this is both a moral and a theological question.

Perhaps there is some truth to all of these questions, but the fact is that congregational members today represent no single homogeneous group asking a single, specific question. In fact, there are many groups represented in the pews. Leander Keck has identified at least seven types of Christians in today's church. (1) The *superpatriots* who will not stand for any criticism of the church. These are the "love it or leave it" Christians. (2) The *cynical citizens* who continue to support the church but sometimes wonder why. They are not sure they believe anything anymore. (3) The *tourists* are those who barely understand the most basic beliefs of the Christian faith. They do a little shopping once in a while, but never buy anything. They are always "just looking." (4) The *resident aliens* are those who believe that religion is a good thing—after all, the Judeo-Christian tradition is what shaped our culture and its moral values. But that is as far as it goes. Jesus was a great man, no more. (5) The *expatriates* are those who bear the scars of earlier religious experiences but have long since moved away from the church. Once in a while they appear in church searching for something they never got. (6) The *reformers* are those who want to change everything about the church. This group includes social activists, some evangelicals, and charismatics. (7) The *church bureaucrats* are primarily clergy who believe they are indispensable. They cannot imagine the church existing without them.[3]

The only group missing from Keck's analysis is the *faithful few* in every church who believe deeply in the Christian faith. This group often represents the core of leadership in any church— people who are active, supportive, and growing in the faith intellectually, spiritually, and morally. They may have questioned their faith at one time as the result of a college course or a crisis in their life. But they have long since decided that Christianity is for them, and their whole life is colored by Christ and his church. This group includes people like the man who still believes in God after his son has been tragically killed. It includes the woman whose final years have been blunted by cancer, but who is nevertheless faithful to the end. It includes those who rarely, if ever, gossip and are almost always positive about the church and those in it because they know how to "speak the truth in love." This group has a larger view of life and of the church than the seven groups named by Keck. Perhaps the *faithful few* is a good name for this group, with the emphasis on *few*. We might also call them the *silent saints*. They are the backbone of the church. A diagram of this faith continuum can help us see these various groups more clearly. At one end of the spectrum I have placed those who have never believed the Christian faith; at the other end are those who are fanatical about it.

Never believed/Once believed/Half-believe/Believe/Fanatical

	expatriates		faithful few	
resident aliens		cynical citizens		superpatriots
	tourists		reformers	

One of the problems with theological language in the pulpit is that so many people hear it in so many different ways. When the superpatriot or the reformer hears the word "sin" on Sunday morning, he or she hears a different meaning than that heard by the resident alien, the cynical citizen, or the expatriate. For the superpatriot, sin may refer to others who are sinful, thus bolstering his or her self-righteousness. For the resident alien, the word may have no effect, or it may be heard as an interesting Christian idea. Actually, this particular word seems to carry more weight with the resident aliens than do other Christian words or doctrines. Witness the attention that Niebuhr received in the academic and political communities with his use of the word. (Even the most casual observer of humanity can readily see that sin is easier to prove than sanctification.) For the cynical citizen or the expatriate, the word "sin" may trigger a false and unnecessary guilt. Unfortunately, none of these people may understand or experience what the preacher, Scripture, or Christian doctrine really intends by use of the word.

What is the problem here? The way you answer this question depends upon whether you are talking about the more secular or the more churchly audience. With the more secular audience (the resident aliens and the tourists), there is at least one problem and one opportunity. The problem, according to Gerhard Ebeling, Paul van Buren, and some "death of God" theologians, is that the word "God" has lost meaning in our time. Our world has lost the sense of God's reality. As a result, the language of faith has become opaque. It has become a "ghetto language"—only comprehensible to theologians. The secular world hears the churchly language with mild curiosity. The most the world can muster in response is a yawn.[4] Perhaps this is the fault of preaching in the modern age, or perhaps it is a fact of the post-Enlightenment age in which we live. Whatever the case, theological language has little effect on resident aliens and tourists when used without some translation, explanation, or illustration. They simply do not hear it.

The opportunity offered by this group is that they *do* in fact want to hear more than clergy may realize. The reason is that people tend to be more religious than we think. I say this very broadly, without statistical proof, but as a statement of conviction: people are ultimately religious. All human beings need a relationship with a "Holy Other" beyond themselves. It takes hard work to be an atheist. Listen to Jacques Ellul: "Being nonreligious involves more intelligence, knowledge, practicality, and method. It calls for virtue, heroism, and greatness of soul. It takes an exceptional personal asceticism to be non-religious."[5] Ellul believes that it takes a strong act of will to achieve this level of atheism. Most people do not have the fortitude to live in total independence. Most cannot live without some "soul supplement."

Ellul further challenges the idea that God has lost all meaning for people today. "Nothing is less certain than that modern man has abandoned God, and that the word God no longer has any meaning for him." The problem of God as an intellectual issue may not be high on the secular person's agenda, but God's presence is still "just as disquieting and certain, just as vitalizing and challenging as ever."[6] Modern humanity may have "come of age," but it is no less interested in the *mysterium tremendum*. If this is not true, then why do young Communists look with fascination and genuine interest at the all-night Easter liturgy of the

Russian Orthodox Church? Why do countless unchurched people in Chicago gather every year to sing Handel's *Messiah?* What are they looking for?

We find these kinds of people throughout the history of the church. It may be an Augustine, that great secular rhetorician, stumbling into Ambrose's church Sunday after Sunday until it finally "took." It may be Frederick Buechner, that gifted novelist, heading to Madison Avenue Presbyterian to hear George Buttrick—or perhaps to hear Christ—searching for something, something not even he expected.

It may be Nathaniel, skeptical about Philip's charismatic excitement and sure that nothing good could come out of *that* town, but interested and curious enough to go see. It may be Cornelius, whose wealth and position would make one question his sincerity. Why does he need religion? He has everything. But Cornelius invites Peter for a private preaching mission. It may be the young bachelor physician, prominent, with a promising career. He will not join the church, but he is there every Sunday. He comes "religiously."

Perhaps Barth is right. Perhaps the question they are asking is, Is it true about God? This may not be the only question, but at the very least it is the primary and most basic question of the secular Christian. It is the question that precedes and overshadows Ogden's, How can I believe in God and live authentically without a sacrifice of intellect?

If the language of faith is unintelligible to the secular Christian, it is not because he or she is uninterested. On the contrary, the secular Christian is quite interested, perhaps more than we think.

There are two problems and at least one opportunity with the churchly audience. One problem is that *the language of faith is opaque.* This is not because the hearer lacks interest, but because the doctrines are not being preached in an intelligible manner. Or perhaps the doctrines have not been preached at all. Such a situation should not be interpreted entirely as an indictment of those in the pulpit. In an attempt to avoid what might be dull, that is, doctrines, we have preached sermons based on Bible stories and an occasional parenetic pericope from Paul. We have sidestepped the great doctrines of the faith because of a few glazed eyes in the audience every time we tried. Or perhaps on occasion we preached the doctrines incorrectly—never on purpose, of course. We preached "works" when Paul meant "grace," so much so that some found they could never live up to the demands and left the church. Some might have wanted something more than a "cheap grace," but may never have heard the obligation of a book like James or the positive use of the law. And so they finally left; the church was too easy for them.

These expatriates and these cynical citizens are, like the secular Christians, searching for something. The language of faith is also opaque to them, not because they are simply worldly, but because they have never heard it or never heard it right.

The second problem with the churchly audience is that *the language of faith is too familiar.* This is Fred Craddock's point in *Overhearing the Gospel.*[7] As in Kierkegaard's nineteenth-century Denmark, so also in Fred Craddock's twentieth-century America has the language of faith lost its impact. The reason is that the cynical citizens, the superpatriots, and, yes, some of the church bureaucrats have heard it too much. The listener is too familiar with the words of faith—not their meaning but their sound. Like Craddock's orphan, the churchly audience is not hungry enough.[8] Unlike the secular Christians, they have stopped searching and long ago decided that they know what they believe. The mere recital of the key words from the pulpit will suffice. It is important that the words be said, but when they have been repeated, life can go on. The ritual recurs Sunday after Sunday.

James Fowler has located this group in what he calls the synthetic-conventional stage, that is, the third stage in the progression of faith development. Here the believer—in addition to a possible adolescent conversion experience, where God has been reimaged in personal terms—relies on a "tacit knowledge" of the Christian faith. The authority for those beliefs comes from parents or some other significant model. The believer has an inherited faith, knowing what the beliefs are, but not the whys, and not really interested in questioning them.[9] In fact, critical reflection causes dissonance. This is reflected in the Catholic woman who says, "Sometimes I just want the priest to tell me what I believe and not raise any doubts about it." This is the classic conformist stage. The superpatriot feels quite at home here. Religious institutions work best with this group because they do not question beliefs. This group is also the prime target for the electronic church. Only when things do not turn out the way they should, or beliefs do not hold up with human experience, do the superpatriots become cynical citizens. Cynical citizens still come to church and stand up Sunday after Sunday reciting the Apostles' Creed, but the words no longer ring true. Perhaps they have become too familiar. They hear the children singing "Jesus Loves Me" and wonder why they do not feel it anymore. They read the Gideon Bible in the motel room, but the pages no longer come alive. God has become a long-lost friend—a friend they once had.

The cynical citizen is right on the edge of Fowler's stage four, the individuative-reflective stage, where some crisis, some traumatic event, has caused inconsistencies to appear in the inherited faith.[10] This may happen in college or with a tragic death or a divorce. Something occurs that shakes one's conventional moorings and causes one either to rethink the faith or leave it altogether. The cynical citizen will become either a reformer or an expatriate. At this point, the person hears the language of faith in a totally new way. He or she listens for its meaning at a deeper level than the person in Fowler's synthetic-conventional stage. For perspective, consider Augustine's *Confessions*. The language of faith is not *too* familiar to this believer. It is usually not radical enough. Because an unbridled self-righteousness usually marks this believer's hearing, it offers the preacher real challenges for interpreting the doctrines of the faith.

The language of faith is rarely too familiar to the faithful few, for they are growing intellectually, spiritually, and morally, and are constantly trying to see new possibilities in living the Christian life. They are not sitting comfortably with an inherited faith nor are they questioning and challenging everything with a self-righteous air.[11]

As we seek to preach doctrine to this mixed church audience, the opportunity that lies before us as Christian preachers is threefold: (1) to challenge those with an inherited faith to see doctrines in a new light; (2) to help those with only a critical faith to begin to heal their spiritual wounds and move on to a deeper knowledge of Christ; (3) to assist the faithful few in their continued growth in the faith.

How will we use theological language to seize this opportunity and make the most of it?

More than a Matter of Style

Theological language, like any other foreign language, is something that has to be learned. In this respect it is no different from technical language for the scientist, medical terminology for the physician, and legal jargon for the lawyer. The language of the Christian is theological language. Some people call it the language of Canaan to distinguish it from the language of Babylon, which is the way the world talks.[12]

The problem for the preacher, simply stated, is, How do we preach theological language? Or, more properly, How do we preach Christ with the help of Christian doctrines?

Three twentieth-century theologians have approached this problem in three different ways. Karl Barth used an approach that made no attempt to translate anything into the language of Babylon. First, Barth believed quite strongly that God was actually speaking when he preached. "Preaching is God's own word."[13] This word is not to be tampered with. "Again it must be emphasized," wrote Barth, "that preaching is not man's attempt to add something to revelation. . . ."[14] Second, Barth's disdain for natural theology turned him away from attempts to translate. In fact, he insisted the preacher should avoid personal experience from his own life as a way of translation.[15] One would assume that this kind of preaching would be dull, abstract, and rote. Not so. Barth walked a narrow line. He preached the Word of God, but never as a bloodless, lifeless exercise in theological lecture. His sermons are full of the lifeblood of the gospel and the tragedy and pathos of human sin as it meets the wonderful gift of God's grace. And Barth preached these kinds of sermons without changing one word of the Christian faith!

Listen how closely Barth walks the line as he talks about the preacher's task:

> Let him speak in the way that is natural to him rather than assuming in the pulpit the cloak of an alien speech. Even the language of the Bible or of poetry as also the ringing tones of an impressive peroration are unsuited to the task he has in hand.
>
> Let him be simple. Those who are engaged in this enterprise should follow the path on which the Bible leads them, should see things as they unfold in actual experience. This will preserve them from displays of doctrinal erudition which are of no great importance. Christian truth is always new when it is set in the context of daily life.[16]

Barth's own sermons are excellent examples of the method he has outlined. He may not translate the gospel by changing the language, but he certainly knows how to preach it. The unlimited grace of God sings throughout his sermons.

Paul Tillich's approach was markedly different. He sought to use language that corresponded to our more psychotherapeutic way of thinking in the twentieth century. Thus, sin became estrangement and salvation became healing. Christ, the new being, "is healing power overcoming estrangement because he himself was not estranged."[17] Even a cursory perusal of Tillich's sermons in *The Shaking of the Foundations, The New Being,* and *The Eternal Now* gives the reader a sense of how well Tillich changed theological language in an effort to speak from the pulpit to modern culture. He made these changes consciously because he believed that there were many more resident aliens, tourists, cynical citizens, and expatriates in our pews than the faithful few. In his opinion, these hearers do not and will not understand theological language that is simply repeated.

One cannot argue with Tillich's strategy. While his sermons are most effective, his approach presents a problem: What happens when that more relevant language itself loses relevance or is not understood by everybody? Tillich did not change the names of any doctrines. Sin is still called "sin." At the same time, he gave us wonderful analogies for doctrines as models for doctrinal preaching.

Emil Brunner explored a middle ground between Barth and

Tillich. With Barth, he wanted to maintain the theological language that had held sway through the centuries; with Tillich, he looked for a way to translate that language so that it spoke to and in the context of human experience. He did this with his famous "point of contact"—that point where the image of God remains in sinful humanity and creates the possibility for the hearing of proclamation. Ian Pitt-Watson believes with Brunner that preachers must search the interpersonal experience and the moral consciousness of hearers in order to bring theological language alive.[18] We are not to repeat the names of doctrines in explanation.

Searching the interpersonal experience of the believer sounds like a rather questionable and mystical experience for any preacher. Exegeting a congregation through regular pastoral visitation is one thing, but how does one search the interpersonal experience of another and relate that to preaching?

I believe Pitt-Watson is on the right track as long as he refers to the common experience of believers. Behind every doctrine there is a common experience of believers that has surfaced again and again and has finally been named "sin" or "sanctification" or "regeneration." Doctrines do not drop out of the sky nor do they represent the emotional euphoria of one person or one congregation or even one age, like the Reformation or the early church. Doctrines have stood the test of time.

Our responsibility as preachers involves finding ways to understand the experience behind the doctrines and helping believers relive that experience, not only intellectually but spiritually and morally. Responsible theologians have always understood this problem. Go back to Augustine, Luther, Calvin, Edwards, Schleiermacher—they always demonstrated the connection between theological ideas and human experience and brought Christian doctrine to bear upon the life of the individual believer. John Smith believes that the analogy of experience is well suited to Christianity because of Christianity's emphasis on a God who comes into history in the form of a man, never in the form of an ideology or a philosophy. Christ is not set forth in a vacuum; he is the Word made flesh who dwelled among us. Smith believes that the only way we can begin to understand the doctrines that speak to the Christ event is by finding the likenesses of it in human experience.[19]

Smith further argues that we cannot preach these doctrines by simply telling the hearers truths, like a scientist who supplies factual information in response to a factual question. We should, rather, "lead another to see, to understand, to apprehend the truth for himself. . . . The aim should be rather to engage the hearer, to 'converse with' him in the hope of creating the possibility of his seeing what the interpreter believes he has seen."[20]

We are now back at our starting point. How do we share the common experience that lies behind the doctrines so that the sermon is more than a surface cognitive experience? Craddock believes we do this by indirect communication, by eliciting capability and action from within the listener, not by giving information. Like a book that gives us distance and room to relate the message to our own experience, a sermon should give us distance and room to maneuver.[21] I once heard George Buttrick preach on what he might say to a Martian about Christian worship. At first I thought that he had lost his mind, but by the end of the sermon I realized that I had "overheard" a doctrinal sermon on Christian worship and had been drawn in to experience it in the process. Preaching that offers the opportunity to overhear gives people space and a chance to hear the gospel at a deeper level.

Tillich answered the question about preaching common experience that lies behind the doctrines by suggesting "identification" and "participation" on the part of the preacher. "We who must communicate the gospel must understand the other. We must somehow participate in [their] existence. . . . We can speak to people only if we participate in their concern, not by condescension but by sharing."[22] A young woman says of another, "I can talk to her because she knows where I am." In preaching, knowing where another is means two things—knowing not only what individuals in your congregation are experiencing but knowing also those universal human experiences that are often named by the doctrines of the Christian faith.

If doctrine is the church's reflection on God's action and our experiences of that action presented in abstract nouns, then our responsibility as preachers is to find ways to reclaim the blood of action that has been drained from these words. What picture does the preacher mean for us to have in our minds when he or she talks of atonement or grace? Edmund Steimle believes that we should translate abstraction into action. "God is active here and now." Something is done, not merely said.[23] The doctrine must be brought to life. Look at the parables, the narratives. Here doctrinal abstraction is given dramatic handling. God comes to us in action, not in dogmas. He comes in a manger, not a proposition. He comes on a cross, not in a conclusion.

According to Steimle, we do not explain faith—we evoke it! That is, through the use of metaphorical language and story that approximates the experience behind the doctrine, we present the living God to our hearers. We do not explain God. We simply offer our hearers the opportunity to meet God. Preaching involves arranging a meeting between God and people. We do not preach about faith; we evoke it.[24] By our use of language, we create the opportunity for this faith encounter to occur in the listeners' consciousness.

Consider, for example, the way a book on logic might discuss the most primitive kind of definition: the ostensive, or pointing, definition, where someone first looked at an animal, pointed, and said "dog." When enough people agreed on that naming, it became a common experience. Nowadays, we still point and name common experiences, like that of listening to a Beethoven symphony and deciding that it is a masterpiece. As Merrill Abbey points out, to do this we must go back again and again—listening to the music and recreating the common experience of that listening—to understand fully how this Beethoven work is a masterpiece, why music theorists believe that, and what difference that makes.[25]

Christian doctrines, of course, are not as concrete as naming a dog or deciding that a piece of music is a great work of art. But when we preach doctrines, we do point and say, "There, now that is what the doctrine of creation is all about." Some might contend that such explicit pointing goes too far, that if you have used your metaphorical language correctly and helped people see their story in the light of the biblical story, the doctrine will emerge implicitly.

I believe, however, that a certain amount of "pointing" is necessary, particularly for those resident aliens, tourists, cynical citizens, and expatriates who often do not catch the subtleties of the well-crafted, sophisticated, narrative sermon. This pointing can occur through one of several different approaches to sermon structure. (1) It can occur with the classic point system, where the preacher says, "The doctrine for today is . . ." and then breaks it down into easily followed points. The danger here is that without effective illustrations, this system can become only explanation. (2) The pointing can occur when the preacher moves from misunderstood doctrine, and conflict resulting from that, to deeper understanding of the doctrine. To do this, the doctrine is named and illustrated in each section of the sermon. (An example is Walter Brueggemann's illustration of the incarnation in which a child cries out in the middle of the night, and the mother comes into the dark room and takes the child into her arms, saying, "It's all right; it's all right, I'm here.") (3) The preacher can use a more metaphorical way of expressing a doctrine like justification, never giving its actual name or form until the end. This approach was once used in a sermon on Rom. 5:1-5, where the Today's English Version translation of "being right with God" was used in place of the Revised Standard Version phrase "justified by faith." In the sermon the preacher explored the problems of saying we must "get right with God" as well as the dimensions of rightness in family, society, and in relationship with God. The preacher also discussed that people try all kinds of ways to make things right, but that what Paul is saying is that people do not have to "get right"; they already are right with God. The very last sentence of the sermon reads: "Therefore, since we are justified by faith, we have peace with God through our Lord Jesus Christ. So that is what being justified means. Thanks be to God."

One of the best ways to do effective pointing in doctrinal preaching is to know the image that lies behind the doctrine, for that image can effectively bring the doctrine to life. Listen to David Buttrick on this point:

The theological method moves from image, metaphor, symbol, and dream, self-awareness, and all those things that have better concrete names, in the anger's flashing moments of vision to which human visions are wont. They move from method, image, metaphor, and symbol to conceptual statements. That is an act of cognitive reduction. The homiletician is a reverse theologian. He too is concerned with the relating of theological statement and nice earthy experience. He is much concerned, but he operates by a kind of process of amplification. Take a faith concept. How do I image it? What are the metaphors? Where are the symbols and the dream talk and the rhythms by which that language formed in what is already formed by lived experience? In one way, the homiletician is a reverse theologian, re-imaging faith.

How are you going to relate the doctrine of atonement to characters in the present world? You going to talk about sacrifice? You sliced any lamb throats lately? You going to talk about slavery? You bought any slaves? The fact is, the old images may not work. How are you going to determine what the new images are? How do we talk faith now? What are the images? Where are they hidden in the new language?[26]

The preacher is a "reverse theologian," seeking to discover new images for the doctrines that already exist. We are not changing the language but the images that express that language. The images will help us point to the experience. This is what Steimle strives toward when he talks about word pictures. A diagram of this homiletical problem might look like this:

Doctrine	Atonement	Providence
Theological Language	God's sacrificial love	God's sustaining care and guidance
Images	Lamb ransomed	Joseph and his brothers
Experience	Being given new life	Trusting God's care

Often, familiar and powerful biblical images, such as the story of Joseph and his brothers, are still effective in attempting to reclaim the experience that lies behind the doctrine. But where are the new images that Buttrick mentions? I believe we can find them in either of two places: (1) the writings of theologians; and

(2) literature, particularly poetry, plays, and novels. Some would also argue here that certain TV shows and movies would be other places. The new images behind the atonement might be found in Eugen Rosenstock-Huessy's description of the cross as reality— the cruciform that makes sense of all the perpetual suffering of our existence.[27] Hans Kung also talks of the image of suffering in his analysis of the meaning of the cross for our time.[28] Perhaps it is the suffering sacrifice of the crucified God in Jürgen Moltmann's thought.[29] Or one might turn to Graham Greene's *The Power and the Glory*. Numerous novels and plays handle the subject of sacrifice and its meaning for modern humanity.[30]

Explanation and Evocation

The different approaches to preaching doctrine can be charted on a homiletical continuum like the one that follows. At one end is the narrative sermon that attempts to explain nothing, but seeks with the use of poetic images to evoke in the hearer the experience implied in the doctrine. At the other end is the teaching sermon that attempts to explain everything. Schleiermacher's analysis of different forms of religious speech can help clarify this continuum. He distinguished between the poetic, the rhetorical, and the didactic. In the poetic form, the speaker creates "images and forms which each hearer completes for himself in his own peculiar way." Because of this the speaker has less control over the response, the actual experience that is generated in the hearer's mind and soul. The rhetorical form of speech is less descriptive, more stimulative, that is, it seeks a "particular definite result." The didactic form achieves the highest possible definiteness and is thus employed for dogmatic propositions in the instruction of believers.[31]

If the purpose of the didactic form is to teach the mind, and the poetic to touch the heart, and the rhetorical to move the will, and all three purposes are important in preaching, then all three should be employed in the preaching of doctrinal sermons. Certainly Edwards's use of the Puritan plain-style approach in his preaching is the best example of this kind of combination. (We will look at Edwards's preaching more specifically in the next chapter.)

The continuum we have been discussing looks like this. It demonstrates the different ways that theological language is used in doctrinal preaching.

Narrative Sermon   Teaching Sermon

Evocation————————————————————Explanation

Poetic   Rhetorical   Didactic

Image   Doctrine

Experience

The reason that responsible doctrinal preaching takes theological language so seriously is that doctrines are the words on which the Christian church has been built. As Ian Ramsey puts it, "'Justification' has been something for which people have been ready to die, and many of the Reformers did."[32] Without the preaching of these doctrines, there would be no spiritual quickening, no moral or spiritual growth, for in every case the doctrines point to Christ.

For Reflection

1. Which of the theologians correctly identifies the question people are asking when they come to church on Sunday morning?

2. Choose a specific Christian doctrine and explore some of the ways you would use theological language in a Barthian sermon and a Tillichian sermon on that doctrine.

3. With the doctrine of sin as the focus, explore ways that you would (a) move from misunderstood notions, to conflict, to a deeper understanding of the doctrine; and (b) present the sermon without the use of the term until the end.

4. With the doctrine of creation as the focus, discuss (a) theological language and (b) old and new images that lie behind it.

5. Study the Robertson sermon (printed in the appendix) to determine the various images he uses to preach specific doctrines.

Further Reading on This Subject

Abbey, Merrill R. *Living Doctrine in a Vital Pulpit*. Nashville: Abingdon Press, 1962: 52–70.

Achtemeier, Elizabeth. *Creative Preaching*. Nashville: Abingdon Press, 1980: 97–103.

Blackwood, Andrew W. *Doctrinal Preaching for Today*. Grand Rapids: Baker Book House, 1975: 17–38, 184–96.

Ebeling, Gerhard. *Introduction to a Theological Theory of Language*. Philadelphia: Fortress Press, 1973: 15–80.

Fawcett, Thomas. *The Symbolic Language of Religion*. Minneapolis: Augsburg Publishing House, 1971: 13–68.

Funk, Robert W. *Language, Hermeneutic, and Word of God*. New York: Harper & Row, 1966: 72–122.

Pitt-Watson, Ian. *Preaching: A Kind of Folly*. Philadelphia: Westminster Press, 1976: 51–63.

Ramsey, Ian. *Religious Language*. London: SCM Press, 1957: 151–86.

Sleeth, Ronald E. *Proclaiming the Word*. Nashville: Abingdon Press, 1964: 72–73, 77–81.

Smith, John. *The Analogy of Experience*. New York: Harper & Row, 1973.

THREE

Doctrine
and the Bible

In a lecture to a homiletics class in the 1950s, James Stewart talked about the preaching of scriptural doctrine. The class had been discussing the problems and possibilities of preaching on 1 Cor. 1:22–24. Stewart suggested that this text offered the preacher a wonderful opportunity to give a sermon on the doctrine of the cross. "For Jews demand signs and Greeks seek wisdom, but we preach Christ crucified, a stumbling block to Jews and folly to Gentiles" (v. 22). Here, Stewart believed, was a text that could be used as the basis of an expository sermon which would present a great doctrine of the church.

When one of the pastors questioned this noted scholar about the preaching of doctrine, Stewart replied, "I think probably the best doctrinal sermons are those which arise in an expository fashion out of the text itself."[1] This is a classic Protestant answer, and one that takes seriously the possibility of doctrinal preaching within the context of a specific scriptural text.

Two other highly respected Protestants, Donald G. Miller and Andrew Blackwood, speak in similar terms of the importance of preaching scriptural doctrine.[2] Miller does so in the context of Paul's great peroration to victory in Rom. 8:28–39. Here he finds the following doctrines: (1) the love of God; (2) atonement; (3) providence; (4) the deity of Christ. They are all in the context of (5) the security of the believer. The preacher would not, of course, attempt all of these in one sermon, and would do well to preach only on one. But the point remains that preaching scriptural doctrine is a legitimate form of Christian preaching.

Doctrinal preaching with the text as a starting point is not only legitimate for many Protestants, but for some it is the only way to preach. Earlier I suggested that there are three possible starting points for sermons: text, doctrine, and issue (question or statement in church or culture). Protestant groups represented generally by those in the Calvinist, Lutheran, and Anabaptist traditions have tended to start with a text in the pulpit, especially when preaching doctrines. Roman Catholics, as well as any others who preach the creeds (like the Dutch Reformed), have tended to begin with the doctrine itself when preaching doctrine from the pulpit. A potpourri of clergy of other denominations have found themselves beginning sermons by addressing an issue. The United Methodists and the United Church of Christ (Congregational strain) primarily comprise this category, but Presbyterians and various others are also included.

Since Vatican II, there has been a resurgence of interest in the Bible among Roman Catholics. The fine, penetrating work of scholars like Raymond Brown, Joseph Fitzmyer, and Roland Murphy, among others, coupled with the renewed emphasis on preaching the lectionary, which has become an ecumenical venture, has brought Scripture to the forefront in Catholic circles. Thus, a shift in interest has moved Catholics closer to Protestants in the area of doctrinal preaching. But traditionally preachers in the Catholic tradition have started with doctrine itself, and many still do.

By combining doctrinal preaching with the text as a starting point, I have reversed the order Brunner uses to locate the three sources of dogmatics. He begins with the polemical element, moves to the catechetical, and finally includes the exegetical, with Augustine's *De doctrina Christiana* and Philipp Melanchthon's *Dogmatics* as examples.[3] Brunner puts these sources in order of their importance for dogmatics; I do so in order of their importance for preaching. By beginning with the exegetical, then moving to the catechetical and polemical, and finally to the apologetic, I have sought to describe the three ways that doctrinal preaching arises and should arise.

I begin with doctrinal preaching based on the biblical text as starting point, and I believe that pastors would do well to follow this approach for two reasons: (1) Beginning with Scripture assures the preacher of remaining close to the original witness to God's revelation in Jesus Christ. All preaching should be grounded in this witness, and there is no better way to be grounded in it than to begin with it. And there is also no better way to avoid preaching one's own opinions. Beginning with Scripture does not mean that the preacher will never veer off target; that happens every Sunday in some pulpits. But the likelihood of it happening is less if serious exegetical work precedes one's preaching. (2) Beginning with Scripture is easier than beginning with a doctrine or an issue. The sheer volume of responsible homework involved in the latter two approaches is staggering, and it increases exponentially when one moves from doctrine to issue. Thus it is almost impossible to preach on doctrines and issues every week. With a text all you have to master is the text itself and the doctrine or doctrines contained therein. Not so with a doctrine or an issue.

Biblical Theology: Old and New

Talk of finding doctrine in Scripture inevitably leads to a discussion of biblical theology. One does not need to rehearse the arguments for or against various forms of biblical theology which have been heard throughout the church. People like Brevard Childs have already done that thoroughly and helpfully.[4]

We are already aware of the dangers and pitfalls that arise with biblical theologies that look for eternal truths—little gems of doctrine within specific, one-verse texts—the dubious gift of nineteenth-century liberalism. We are aware of the "doctrines of the Bible" books by people like William Evans and B. B. Warfield,[5] which draw together various texts and organize them under headings according to the author's theological bent, with minimal sensitivity to biblical criticism. These books become motif studies, with little more than proof texts for support, while being untrue to the historical and literary context of the biblical text. We know also the more sensitive biblical critics like Rudolf Bultmann, Millar Burrows, Walter Eichrodt, and Gerhard von Rad, among

others, who have sought to be true to scripture while discussing
its theological themes.[6] While Burrows and others did not attempt
to form a system which was extrabiblical, that was sometimes the
result. James Barr's criticism of the biblical theology movement
of the 1940s to the 1960s is well taken.[7] The exponents of biblical
theology were, according to Barr, taking biblical criticism seriously, but not the biblical text itself. And as Childs points out:

> The Bible does not function in its role as canon to provide a collec-
> tion of eternal ideas, nor is it a handbook of right doctrine, nor a
> mirror of man's religious aspirations. . . .
>
> Any sensitive reading of the Bible reveals that seldom does the
> Bible move within broad, abstract categories such as the doctrine of
> man, sin, or the "last things." Rather, the Psalms reflect on man in
> his glory and man in his insignificance within the world (Psalm 8).[8]

Childs understands the need for theological interpretation and
exegesis in preaching. He recognizes the theological themes
present in the Bible that find their way into the workroom of the
theologian and the faith of the believer. But he believes that these
themes can emerge in modern scholarship and modern preaching
in a way that is true to the scriptural and churchly contexts.

Childs's model for this emergence is represented by the great
theologians of the past, specifically Augustine, Luther, and
Calvin.[9] Look at their commentaries and sermons. The Bible was
not only for the mind but for the soul, and it was a challenge to the
will. These precritical exegetes and preachers may have lacked
precision in biblical criticism, but their theological interpretations
struck home and brought the Bible to the heart of the believer.
Read Calvin's commentaries. Look at Luther on Romans. There
is a richness in these writings that is hard to beat. These are the
models for theological exegesis.

What Calvin and Luther and Barth were able to do so well was
hold in tension the original scriptural context and the churchly, or
canonical, context. Biblical theology that deals only with scriptural context is *descriptive;* it leaves to the dogmatician the task
of constructing a theology normative for the faith. Biblical theol-

ogy that is *normative* takes the churchly context and the faith of the believer into account, while at the same time staying close to the thought patterns and forms of Scripture.

The danger of being only descriptive in biblical theology and doctrinal preaching is that one never addresses the heart of the believer. Like an agnostic history of religions expert or master of biblical word study, one can take a text apart but never put it back together for a congregation. There is nothing more frustrating for a preacher, and subsequently for the parishioners, than to try to make sense out of a sermon informed by commentaries that reduce the living witness of God's revelation to history, literature, and linguistic analysis.

The danger of being only normative without the descriptive grounding is that the biblical theologian and the preacher can turn their interpretations and sermons into spiritual and moral exhortations that have no connection with the biblical witness. If various forms of textual preaching that Fosdick reacted against have become the heirs of the descriptive approach to biblical theology in doctrinal preaching, then various forms of topical preaching have become the heirs of the normative approach. Responsible biblical theology and doctrinal preaching seek to employ both descriptive and normative approaches, both scriptural and churchly contexts.

Let us take this one step further by comparing the tasks of the biblical theologian and the dogmatic theologian. The biblical theologian engages in both descriptive and normative analysis. Some scholars tend to focus on one type of analysis more than the other; for instance, the Harvard school tends to do more descriptive philological study, while the Yale school focuses more on the normative, although Childs himself represents a good combination of both. The biblical theologian who helps the doctrinal preacher the most not only investigates Scripture in its own setting, as heard by ancient Israel and the early church, but investigates the theology that informs a certain text, for instance, the theology of Second Isaiah or the theology of Paul. The biblical theologian is not interested in speculative reasoning or a specific theological system.[10] As a believing inquirer, the biblical theologian attempts to bring forth the deeper theological meaning of the text, knowing that Scripture is the grounding, the root, the starting point for most of the major doctrines of the Christian faith. The task is not to trace the doctrines' subsequent development but to examine and understand their roots.

The dogmatic theologian, also a believing inquirer, shares the task of theology with the biblical theologian, but from a different angle, with a different agenda in mind. The biblical theologian works out from Scripture as he or she investigates the genesis of various doctrines. The dogmatic theologian starts with the doctrines of the church and looks back to the biblical witness to examine the beginnings of these well developed doctrines, indeed, the foundations of the Christian faith. Therefore, biblical and dogmatic theologians have a common meeting ground in Scripture.

Form and Redaction Criticism

Doctrinal preachers who seek to preach doctrine by starting with the text are helped in many ways by the biblical theologian. The biblical theologian helps them avoid the pitfalls of the nineteenth-century liberals (preaching eternal truths), the Warfields (lapsing into proof texting), and the adherents of the mid-twentieth-century biblical theology movement (forcing the Bible into various systems). Moreover, the biblical theologian does not retreat from theology into an objectively helpful but spiritually arid philological, archaeological, and historical approach, but instead reaps the fruit of form and redaction criticism, which sharpens not only textual preaching but doctrinal preaching that uses the text as starting point.

How can form criticism help doctrinal preaching? By reminding us that the Bible presents many genres in various forms of literature. Each literary type functions in a different way, often with a different theological purpose. As Donald Gowan suggests:

> Law is not functioning in the same areas of life as saga, and its message is not the same. If we look to both of them for predictions of the Messiah or for moral examples or spiritual insights, if we

approach each of them hoping to distill two, three, or four predictable points of doctrine, then we do violence to their quite specific kind of message. . . .[11]

Since we know that saga, historical texts, law, wisdom, and prophetic texts are all different in the Old Testament—just as narrative, controversy-pronouncement, parable, and Pauline parenesis are different in the New Testament—we are called to preach doctrine with an eye to these limitations and opportunities.

For example, if we realize that one of the purposes of historical texts (like the succession narratives found in 2 Samuel and 1 and 2 Kings and 1 and 2 Chronicles) is to help us see our place in the continuing history of God and God's people, then the doctrine of providence is more in order with these texts than the doctrines of judgment, mercy, and even hope, which would tend to appear in doctrinal sermons on prophetic passages. As in every other case, each text would have to be examined for its specific doctrinal potential.

Sagas are not so easily analyzed. Sagas are shorter units of folk literature, with a more private than public nature (unlike historical texts). The story of Jacob at the Jabbok is an example of a saga. Sagas include various theological themes which do not easily work themselves into sermons on a single, specific doctrine. Jacob at the Jabbok could deal with sin, guilt, repentance, forgiveness, and reconciliation, but all of this in one sermon would be formidable. Again, the form of a saga helps us decide. It helps us take the focus off Jacob, Esau, and ourselves, and place the focus on God. We are only players on the stage of this divine drama. Listen to von Rad:

God is everywhere the real narrative subject, so to speak, of the saga—or rather, its inner subject; men are never important for their own sakes but always as objects of the divine activity; as those who both affirm and deny God and his command.[12]

The saga of Jacob at the Jabbok tells us more about God than about ourselves. God is the one who brings direction to our lives, who puts Jacob into the position of leadership despite his self-centeredness. God is the one who calls us up short in the midst of our sin. God is the one who gives blessing. God is the one who brings about restoration. The passage is about God.

Short stories are much more freewheeling than sagas. Again, God is the focus, but there is an even stronger emphasis on our freedom within the larger divine providence. Short stories are longer than sagas and always have a beginning, a middle, and an end. Jonah is the classic example of this form. Short stories resist distillation. They want to live in their own form. They resist reduction to doctrinal points. Even in a doctrinal sermon, a retelling of the story with the tone and color of the genre in mind often does it more justice. See the sermon on Jonah in the appendix for an example. It attempts to allow theological themes to come to the fore without doing harm to the form of the short story.

The same could be said for parable as form. Parables are often thought to be devoid of theology. They are used as moral exhortations, for example, to be good soil, as in the Parable of the Sower, or to help the poor, as in the Good Samaritan, [13] or to forgive your errant son, as in the Prodigal Son. But in each a deeper theological point is being made. These are not little moral lessons but deeply theological statements with a twist that leaves hearers in a state of cognitive and emotive dissonance. They are about the effectual power of the seed (God's Word); the healing love of the *real* Good Samaritan, whose love is never calculating, who finds a neighbor at every turn; the unbelievable grace of God that angers, threatens, and challenges all of us pharisaical older-brother types with a call to repentance. The parables carry rich lodes ready to be mined for doctrinal preaching. But beware—like the short stories and sagas of the Old Testament, they too resist reduction to carefully and logically deduced points. If you do use points, give the whole sermon the flavor of parable, including especially the surprise at the end.

Doctrinal preachers who begin with a text are actually helped more by redaction criticism than by form criticism. In redaction criticism the emphasis is not so much on the preliterary genres, the separate functions of separate units of Scripture, but on the theological intention of the various editors of the Bible. One of the real dangers of some forms of biblical theology is their attempt to unify Scripture into one theological system. Redaction criticism argues that the Bible resists that process because of its many writers and thus its many theologies. A single unifying system blurs the distinctiveness of Scripture.

Attempts at forming a New Testament theology must reckon with the pluralism of theological perspectives in the New Testament. We can no longer talk of the synoptics, the Pauline, and the Johannine theologies. Matthew, Mark, and Luke-Acts must be taken separately. Authentic Pauline material must be distinguished from pseudo-Pauline writings. Early writings of Paul must be distinguished from his great letters and his captivity letters.[14] Hebrews, the pastorals, 1 and 2 Peter, and James have their own say as separate from the Johannine writings. Each book has its own integrity. To say "The Bible says . . . " in a doctrinal sermon—or any sermon—becomes almost ludicrous in the light of redaction criticism findings.[15]

If each redactor or editor places his own theological imprint on the story of Jesus, and Paul has his say with various struggling New Testament churches, it becomes more and more difficult to talk of the New Testament doctrine of atonement. Imagine the differences as one ranges between Romans and Hebrews.

The biblical theologian could despair in the presence of such pluralism. Such apparent theological chaos seems to lead only to cacophony, as if each member of the orchestra has begun playing whatever he or she likes. Fortunately, this is not the case. The pluralism, in fact, adds richness, just as the flutist, the bassoonist, and the cellist add richness to an orchestra by making different sounds and by playing different notes at different speeds and different volumes all during the same piece. Different New Testament theologies all point to Christ. Sometimes they do this in dissonance, but this adds richness to the whole. The message is many faceted.

Our responsibility as doctrinal preachers who start with a text is not to say everything there is to say about atonement (if that happens to emerge as a doctrine in the text on which we are about to preach), but to say what the author of Hebrews has said, or what Paul has said here in the context of this particular letter. At least this makes the task a little bit easier. Now I only have to deal with one writer's theological angle on this particular doctrine in this particular text. Since we cannot hope to preach the whole gospel every Sunday, we should make no excuses for offering a good look at one side of it this Sunday. To change the musical metaphor to a more visual one, the gospel is like a great gem that cannot be appreciated completely in a single glance, but must be turned slightly, week after week. Only after a time do we begin to see it in all its brilliance.

Doctrine and the Lectionary

One way to look at this many faceted gospel is to preach the lectionary on a weekly basis. The lectionary passages present the doctrines of the gospel in all of its richness. Since 1969, when the Roman Catholic church completed its *Ordo Lectionum Missae*, Anglican, Lutheran, Reformed, and United Methodist churches have joined Catholics in one of the most ecumenical ventures ever adopted—the weekly use of a common lectionary. This unified approach represents the most organized attempt in the history of the church to communicate the gospel to the world. Lectionary helps have abounded, each offering balanced exegetical, theological, and homiletical suggestions to the modern-day preacher. Some, like Robert Crotty, Gregory Manly, and Reginald Fuller, attempt to balance the descriptive and normative approaches to biblical theology.[16] Others, like Gerard Sloyan, focus more on the former.[17] The Proclamation series offer a blend by having two separate writers for most of the books.[18] Thus, the modern-day preacher's desk is full of all kinds of commentaries which open the biblical text into expository and doctrinal sermons.

But not the full biblical text. The lectionary, as many have found out, is a canon within a canon. A very careful, selective process has brought together this assortment of texts. The preacher must remember that it is a selection, and the same one every three years. It is more condensed than the Reader's Digest Condensed Bible. It is more selective than the *lectio continua* approach of some Protestant preachers, who begin at the beginning of a book and go straight through, or the faithful laity who read the Bible from cover to cover. The lectionary is admittedly *lectio selecta*. It makes no apologies about that, and well it should not. The lectionary is one of the best things to happen to Christian preaching for centuries. Of course, some form of lectionary has been around since the first Jewish synagogue, but only recently have so many begun to use the lectionary, and jointly so.

The fact remains that the lectionary provides for only a selection of readings, which means that something has to be left out. Yes, whole books of the Bible are missing: Judges, Ruth, Ezra, Esther, Obadiah, Nahum, Haggai, and the Psalms in the Old Testament, and 2 and 3 John and Jude in the New Testament. When you think of the scope of the whole Bible, that is not bad. After all, it takes more than three years to read through the Bible one chapter a day. But the Psalms are missing, as well as whole sections of other books. Imagine the rich doctrinal material not being touched if a preacher stays with the lectionary alone.

While the lectionary does not cover all doctrines, it does cover most of the major ones, since theological themes coincide with seasons to direct the choice of certain passages. Some doctrines, however, have been omitted. When using the lectionary, we should ask ourselves what doctrine is included and what theological angle on that doctrine is being communicated through the lectionary by a certain Gospel or epistle writer's view. On the whole, the lectionary has done a responsible job of giving fair theological representation. Witness the great range of epistle texts during the season of Lent across all three years. There are other examples as well. But the lectionary is not without critics on this score. Sloyan finds the lectionary lacking in specific areas. "The lectionary is all but silent on the marvel of creation and the paradox of the grandeur and wretchedness of human life," he says. "It uses none of the great nature psalms as a sustained reading, and from the riches of Job calls only on 7:1–4, 6–7 and

38:1, 8–11.''[19] Sloyan rightly questions the meager use of Job and Ecclesiastes. There three texts in the lectionary "stand alone in representing the human wrestling with tedium, purposelessness, and frustration conveyed by those books." The biggest problem for Sloyan is the heavily christocentric nature of the lectionary.

> There is, in a word, a kind of nervousness throughout the lectionary that not every problem raised by the Hebrew scriptures may be seen as solved by the incarnation, death, and resurrection of Jesus Christ. "Christ is the answer" would seem to be the chief interpretative principle behind the selections, but with something bordering on an anticipated Parousia. One suspects that the overall performance might give a certain pleasure to St. Paul, but at sensitive points disappoint him deeply. . . . Congregations are being protected from the insoluble mystery of God by a packaged providence, a packaged morality, even a packaged mystery of Christ.[20]

Sloyan's analysis is trenchant and telling. Beginning with the text of the lectionary Sunday after Sunday will offer a doctrinal stance that is strongly christocentric but weak on the deep human anguish and frustration presented in the Old Testament; it is also strong on providence but weak on creation. Preachers should use the lectionary fully aware of these doctrinal limitations.

One additional note of caution. Since during the seasons of Epiphany and Pentecost the editors of the lectionary have made a conscious attempt to create a *lectio continua* in the epistle selections, you will not find a clear, uniform doctrinal theme across the three lessons. Do not attempt to force one.

Ten Questions

Once you have selected a passage to preach, either through the lectionary, through *lectio continua*, or through your own time-tested method, you need to proceed to the exegesis and construction of the sermon. You have done some of the exegetical homework, and, as with Acts 2, have found at least one theological theme (and perhaps many more). It is now time to begin answering specific questions that will lead to a doctrinal sermon. These ten questions are not exhaustive; still they move us in the right direction as we seek to do responsible doctrinal preaching while retaining the integrity of the biblical witness.

To bring these questions into focus, let us use them to examine a specific text: "Likewise the Spirit helps us in our weakness; for we do not know how to pray as we ought, but the Spirit himself intercedes for us with sighs too deep for words. And he who searches the hearts of men knows what is the mind of the Spirit, because the Spirit intercedes for the saints according to the will of God" (Rom. 8:26–27).

1. What doctrines appear in this text? Several, to be sure. In general, we would name the following: Spirit, sin ("in our weakness; for we do not know how to pray as we ought"), prayer, omniscience ("he who searches the hearts of men knows what is the mind of the Spirit"), the immanence and transcendence of God, and the will of God, or providence.

2. How do these doctrines fit into the context of this book of the Bible? Sandwiched between Paul's song of hope and his ringing peroration on victory, "No in all these things we are more than conquerors . . ." comes this peculiar statement on prayer. It helps bring to a close Paul's resonating theological masterpiece, as chapters 9—11 deal with God's chosen people, and chapter 12 begins the ethical section. The "groaning," or "sighing," continues from the previous passage (8:22–23), which caused Sangster to preach on the "three groans": creation, ourselves, and God.

The Spirit here in these verses is functioning in only one way. At other places in Romans (particularly in other places in chapter 8), we find that the Spirit makes us free from the law of sin and death, dwells in us, quickens our mortal bodies, enables us to control the flesh, and makes us children of God—heirs. But here the Spirit intercedes for us in prayer.

3. How do these doctrines fit into the context of the whole canon? Widening the scope in this way brings the larger picture of the Spirit before us. We know from Paul and other writers that the Spirit convicts us, justifies us, regenerates and sanctifies us, and makes real our prayer privileges. This last function is the focus of our text. Thus, a doctrinal sermon on this text need not cover all the dimensions of the meaning of "Spirit." Neither should it attempt to bring in the Johannine concepts of the Spirit as teacher and as comforter.

In the same way, the doctrine of prayer being discussed here is not the same as that in the Gospels when the disciples say, "Lord, teach us to pray." Here the emphasis is more on our weakness, our deep hurt, longing, and need, than on our desire to learn how to pray.

A much more important theological point is brought to light, however, when trying to discover the real reason behind these doctrines of Spirit and prayer. Why does God help us this way in our weakness? Because it is the nature of our God to come to us, to assist us. It has been so from the beginning, when God called Abraham and lifted him up, when God brought Israel out of Egypt and delivered the people from exile in Babylon. It is God's nature to come in human form among us, the "Word made flesh," and to give us Jesus' life on our behalf. The doctrines in this passage are held together by this one biblical word of grace—it is God's nature to come to us.

4. *Does the form of Scripture affect our interpretation of these doctrines?* Up to now, we have been making redaction-critical assessments. This question pushes us to consider the form of Scripture in Paul. Since the New Testament form-criticism of Martin Dibelius and Rudolf Bultmann deal primarily with the forms found in the Gospels, this question is not as crucial for the Pauline material. Paul's writings fall into one of four categories: (1) theological assessment, as in Romans; (2) correction and challenge, as in Corinthians and Galatians; (3) pastoral comfort, as in 1 Thessalonians; and (4) love letter, as in Philippians (which includes a Christ hymn, 2:1–11). Some would add a fifth category of high christological grandeur, depending on their view of Paul's authorship of Ephesians and Colossians.

It is clear that we have here the form of theological assessment, but it is also clear that the text we are analyzing participates in the crescendo of Romans 8 which begins, "There is therefore now no condemnation for those who are in Christ Jesus." The form may not affect our interpretation, but it should influence our presentation.

5. *What is the major theological thrust of this passage?* We have already answered that question in part. God comes to us with help in prayer through the Spirit. This is another ringing word about God's prevenient and unmerited grace.

6. *Which doctrines in this passage are more directly related to the theological thrust of the passage and which are more peripheral?* The Spirit, in its limited function of helping us with prayer, certainly relates directly. Dealing extensively with the Spirit beyond this scope moves away from the theological thrust. Sin, demonstrated by our weakness and our inability to pray as we ought, is only peripherally related to the main thrust. The omniscience of God is not the main doctrine either. A sermon on that would be off target. The will of God is only significant in understanding the meaning of right prayer. God chooses for us what is best. "According to the will of God" should not end up as a sermon on providence. Certainly vv. 28–30 point to that doctrine explicitly. But the key here is staying with the main theological thrust of the passage in consideration.

7. *What questions would your congregation or culture ask about this passage? Where are the pressure points, the conflict(s)?* This passage does not answer the question, Why do we need to pray in the first place? It assumes that those reading it or hearing it are Christians who are already struggling with the meaning of existence and the meaning of right prayer. We come hurting, searching for some help. We have already looked into ourselves too much. We have tried jogging, meditation, success. All fall short. Looking into ourselves has not brought deep happiness—only the surface variety. We come to church, and the preacher tells us to look to God in prayer. That seems an odd thing to do. We have tried from childhood by the bedside, but gave up long ago out of weakness; we just do not know how to do it. Paul says that the Spirit helps. But how does the Spirit help? It all sounds very mysterious. Why does God help?

8. *Which doctrines tend to fit those pressure points best?* There

are, of course, other possible questions and pressure points, but these will suffice for this example. The doctrine of sin is looming larger than it was earlier as an entry point in our consideration of this passage. We do not know how to pray as we ought. We are a people in need of help—help beyond ourselves. God brings this help in the Spirit, the answer to our problem. But why does God do so? Why would God care for me? Back to the theological thrust: it is God's nature to do so. Sin and grace become the doctrines that deal with the pressure points best. How the Spirit helps must be answered with the consideration of images.

9. *What image is used to bring this doctrine into focus, and what is the modern analogy for this image?* The action in this passage comes with the Spirit interceding for us with "sighs too deep for words." There is actually no image presented in this passage to bring the concept of intercession to life for the hearer. Therefore, an image needs to be constructed that will get close to the thought of the passage and the doctrine of God's prevenient love through the Spirit in the act of prayer. For example, think of a lawyer pleading your case before the jury. Like the Spirit, the lawyer knows what you want to say better than you do. Another image that could be considered is the presidential aide who gives you access to the president so that you may report to him or her the nature and extent of the flooding in your home town, and the extent of the help needed immediately.

Perhaps this next image comes even closer. The head of a major American denomination was speaking in Egypt with the help of an interpreter. At one point the interpreter went on and on, obviously saying much more than the church leader had said. When the interpreter stopped, the church leader asked, "What did you say?" The interpreter replied, "You were talking about God's love and God's care, but what you were saying wasn't very helpful, so I used Psalm 23 to explain. I believe I got the point across a lot better than you."

Whatever image you use, the idea of Rom. 8:26–27 is that we do not really know how to pray or what to pray for. We pray much too selfishly and on too small a scale. As Luther suggests, we ask for silver when God wants to give us gold. In prayer we mutter and mumble, sometimes in sighs too deep for words, but the Spirit gets the point across a lot better than we do. Thanks be to God for that!

10. What structure will you use to preach the doctrine in this passage? The sensitive preacher will always keep in mind the form of Scripture itself. Does it offer signals as to how best to preach the doctrine? Aside from that consideration, many structural approaches always present themselves.

On this text, one could preach two large points. (1) We do not know how to pray as we ought (giving the evidence and the reason for this). (2) The Spirit helps us by interceding with God (offering examples of how this happens).

Another approach might be a more dialogical structure which would present several arguments, rebuttals, and doctrinal statements using a problem-reason-solution motif. The outline would follow this pattern:

Problem: We are miserable (give examples).
Reason: We look into ourselves too much.
Solution: We look to God.
Problem: Looking to God does not work because we cannot look to God. We certainly have tried.
Reason: We are weak in the flesh.
Solution: The Spirit helps us (show how with an image).
Reason: It is the nature of our God to come to us with help (prevenient grace), to be with us (incarnation), to intercede for us (atonement).

Whatever system you employ, be sure that it moves, that it is not static. Make sure it proceeds from one place to another. For some that may mean going from known to unknown, from present experience to gospel reality, which is often in conflict with present experience. For others it may mean progressing through the text. Make it dynamic—that is the key. In addition, whatever structure you employ, make sure it is clear and simple. Be sure that it makes the Bible passage's main doctrine and theological thrust come alive in the sermon. Since structure is often a place where sermons make it or break it, we turn now to four approaches to preaching doctrine from a text which have stood the test of time.

Four Structural Approaches:
Barth, Calvin, Edwards, and Stewart

For years pastors, seminary students, and laity have read the writings of theologians for their theology. But how many have read these same theologians' sermons to see how they present their theology to the person in the pew? Tillich may be hard to manage in his *Systematic Theology,* but what happens when he preaches? What happens when you turn from Barth's *Church Dogmatics* to his sermons delivered in Basel prison?

My experience has been that the great theologians preach with clarity, simplicity, profundity, and pastoral sensitivity. This is especially true of the theologians I have chosen in this chapter to illustrate four approaches to preaching doctrine with Scripture as a starting point.

I begin with *Karl Barth,* because in some senses he offers the simplest system. Barth loved to preach. Like Dietrich Bonhoeffer, he was torn between pulpit and podium, between sanctuary and classroom. It is well known that his theological writings grew out of his preaching—its anguish, challenge, and joy.

When he preached, Barth always attempted to go deep into the pain of the human experience and deep into the wells of the gospel. He sought "an answer to the cry of the soul not for truths but for the Truth, not for solutions but for the solver. . . ."[21] Barth aimed for encounter between believer and God. To give his congregation anything less was to leave them shortchanged, to send them away empty-handed when they had come with great hunger.

Barth attempted to create this encounter as simply as he could. He did so by preaching one-verse texts, building the sermon by taking one word or phrase at a time. H. Grady Davis has summarized this sequential structure by giving the outline of Barth's sermon "Repentance," based on Matt. 11:28, "Come unto me, all ye that labour and are heavy laden" (KJV).

1. Jesus calls us to turn to him, to God, to our own hidden, unknown center and source. Repentance is this turning. "Come unto me."
2. Jesus' call must be distinguished from all other calls, including the church's call. "Unto *me*."
3. Jesus alone is for all men. "All ye."
4. Jesus alone seeks us at the point of labor, burdens, failures, wrongness, death. "That labour and are heavy laden."
5. Jesus alone asks of us nothing but to come. "Come unto me."[22]

Notice how Barth stays close to the text, how he allows the text to give him not only content but structure. In addition, notice how he preaches on repentance, but only touches one side of it. As Davis points out, Barth feels no compulsion to examine repentance from every angle. His doctrinal sermon stays within the confines of this text.

Barth's sermon on the text "Nevertheless I am continually with thee;—thou dost hold my right hand" (Ps. 73:23, KJV) moves through that verse in a similar way. The sermon deals with the doctrines of humankind and God. Barth's theological anthropology is brought into contact with the richness of God's grace as he brings the text to life word by word, phrase by phrase.

John Calvin was an extemporaneous preacher who nevertheless engaged in careful mental preparation before he preached. Like Barth, he believed in the power of preaching and its importance. Also like Barth, he preached through a text phrase by phrase, but he often used whole pericopes instead of one-verse texts. With Calvin there was little distinction between doctrinal and expository preaching. Every sermon was both. Calvin placed each sermon within its canonical context. As he opened the text, he brought the pertinent doctrines to bear on the needs of the congregation. His preaching was never merely an intellectual exercise.

Sometimes Calvin would focus on one doctrine, as in his sermon "The Privilege of Prayer" on 1 Tim. 2:8. Often he would attack heretical positions in polemical fashion, as in "Pure

Preaching of the Word" on 2 Timothy 2:16–18. Occasionally many doctrines would surface to serve a larger theological thrust, as in "The Deity of Jesus Christ" on John 1:1–5, where in addition to the incarnation we hear about the Trinity, creation, providence, humankind, and sin. Time kept Calvin from mentioning others. Toward the end of that sermon he himself says, "That is what the Gospel writer wished to indicate. I omit other things because time does not permit us to speak of them further, and already I have spoken too long."[23]

Here, at least, is an honest preacher. And yet his tendency to attempt too many doctrines at once caused his sermons on occasion to sound too large for one hearing. In this respect, Calvin is not a good model for doctrinal preachers. Despite the fact that he sometimes uses too many doctrines, it must be said that he does draw the doctrines from the text at hand. "For we are sure that such as seek God's honour and their own salvation will perceive in reading the sermons that their author had no other doctrine than is contained in the Epistle. . . ."[24] One thing is clear: Calvin's sermons are not theological lectures for the erudite. They are sermons that teach the believer and comfort the troubled soul, and they do so with scriptural doctrine.

Jonathan Edwards was a man of his age. Historically, he brought together the appeal to the intellect represented by the Puritans and the rationalists, like Charles Chauncey of Boston, and the appeal to the heart represented by Charles and John Wesley, Philipp Spener, August Francke, and James Davenport. This combination of order and ardor in Edwards demonstrated his support for the validity of religious experience and the need for that experience to be tied to understanding.

Epistemologically, Edwards follows John Locke, who believed that there were no innate ideas and that understanding depended on sensation or experience. To have the idea of seven, you have to have had the experience of counting to seven. But Edwards goes beyond Locke by distinguishing between people as they are by nature and spiritual people. We·acquire certain notions naturally: color, sound, warmth, guilt, misery, and sin. But only an extraordinary work of the Holy Spirit brings about the sense of the loveliness and sweetness of God's grace. To talk to people in their natural state about these things is to talk nonsense. Without the experience of grace, you cannot have the idea of grace. Only God can bring this about by the Spirit.

Edwards's thinking led him to a religion of the heart which anticipated that of Kierkegaard. An idea was not only for the head but for the heart, which meant that the sermon must touch the emotions of the believer in order for the truth of doctrines to be transmitted. Language, then, was very important to Edwards, and he used it very carefully; he also knew its limitations. Only the Spirit of God could really bring about a religious experience. The preacher's words merely created a proper environment for the Spirit's work.

Rhetorically, Edwards was influenced indirectly by Peter Ramus, who had reordered Aristotelian rhetoric, and William Perkins, who, following Ramus, wrote "The Art of Prophesying" and thereby influenced what was to be called the Puritan plain style approach to preaching. Here sermons looked more like lawyers' briefs. The beginning opened the biblical text in short exposition; the middle section was laid out in a series of reasons and proofs; the final section was application. The sermons of Edwards's time followed this pattern slavishly. Exposition-doctrine-application or text-doctrine-use.

Theologically, Edwards followed Calvin. The sovereignty of God was set alongside humanity's dependence. Despite the bad press that "Sinners in the Hands of an Angry God" has gotten, Edwards did not use doctrine to scare "the hell" out of people. He always preached the unlimited power of God's grace. Doctrine was preached as a corrective for two sins—pride and despair.

Edwards's sermon "The Excellency of Christ" is a classic example of the Puritan plain-style approach which takes a text, in this case Rev. 5:5–6, and opens it through exposition-doctrine-application.[25] In reading this sermon, one notices immediately the Ramist method of dichotomy in the doctrinal section as Edwards talks of the person of Christ as infinite glory and lowest humility, infinite majesty and transcendent meekness, and the like. One also notices the number of doctrines he brings forth from this text. His Christology includes incarnation, atonement, love, justice, and holiness. There is no attempt to change the language, but the images of lion and lamb do make the doctrines come alive amid Edwards's eloquence.

Some still preach with the Puritan plain-style approach. Its strength lies in its simplicity and clarity. Its weakness comes with its predictability and potential dullness. Edwards may have been predictable, but he was never dull. Despite his apparently tedious, monotonous style of delivery, with no eye contact, his preaching kept his congregation spellbound. There is a quiet passion and vigor that breathes through his sermons as he opens the biblical texts into doctrines that helped his hearers not only know who they were as Christians, but live the Christian life.

We began this chapter with *James Stewart,* and we will close it with him. Stewart was a great preacher; that is a fact. There was more to his greatness than his Scottish accent. Some have tried to get by on accent or affect alone, and have only made fools of themselves. There was more to Stewart's greatness than his New Testament scholarship. Certainly that helped. Stewart saw the big picture when he preached. He saw the broad strokes of the gospel next to the bloodstained face of the world. He saw Calvary's pain and Easter's victory. Read his sermons and you will see.

Stewart's approach to structure was eclectic. Sometimes he followed the pattern of Barth and Calvin and simply let the text unfold naturally. Other times he imposed points on a text, but only those that the text in a canonical context suggested. On occasion he employed a dialogical approach which found him wrestling with a text and with the congregation's questions and conflicts as well. His sermon "The Power of His Resurrection" follows this pattern.[26] Here is its basic outline, although the sermon resists this kind of distillation.

Sermon: The Power of His Resurrection

I. Introduction. Resurrection is the symbol for Christianity. There is no darkness that it does not illuminate. Test and see. (He gives examples.)

II. Scripture Reading
III. Body
    A. It was God who resurrected Christ; he will raise us up, too.
       1. We don't believe it, do we?
       2. The early Christians did. They turned the world upside down.
       3. We are still slow to take it in.
       4. The New Testament writers will not accept that denial.
    B. Before resurrection can happen for us, we are called to surrender.
IV. Conclusion

This is the final example of a preacher who begins with a text but preaches doctrine in the pulpit. The purpose of this chapter has been to explore the problems and possibilities of preaching Christian doctrine while starting with a biblical text. I have argued that this is the best way to begin a doctrinal sermon as long as one avoids the pitfalls of older approaches to biblical theology and takes advantage of the benefits of form and redaction criticism. Doctrinal preaching that begins with a text and sticks with it is assured of being grounded in the biblical witness to Jesus Christ.

For Reflection

1. Choose a text from the lectionary and answer the following questions:
    a. What doctrines appear in this text?
    b. How do these doctrines fit into the context of this book of the Bible?
    c. How do these doctrines fit into the context of the whole canon?
    d. Does the form of Scripture affect your interpretation of these doctrines?
    e. What is the major theological thrust of this passage?
    f. Which doctrines in this passage are more directly related

to the theological thrust of the passage and which are more peripheral?

2. Having answered these questions, determine what questions your congregation or culture would ask about the passage (keeping in mind the various audiences we address, as discussed in chapter 2), where the pressure points occur, and how the doctrine or doctrines relate to those questions and points of conflict.

3. Determine what image is used to bring this doctrine into focus, what the modern analogy is for this image, and how, as a reverse theologian, you will employ it.

4. Determine what structure you will use to preach the doctrine in this passage. Choose from the following possibilities:

   a. A simple, straightforward point system.

   b. A Barthian or Calvinist approach which takes one or two verses and uses the words or phrases of the verse as parts of the structure.

   c. A Puritan plain-style approach like that used by Jonathan Edwards.

   d. A dialogical moving approach which allows the congregation's questions to emerge, similar to the Jonah sermon in the appendix. Stewart's sermon is a combination of point and dialogue systems.

Further Reading on This Subject

Blackwood, Andrew W. *Doctrinal Preaching for Today*. Grand Rapids: Baker Book House, 1975: 125–37.

Carl, William J., III. "Planning Your Preaching: A Look at the Lectionary," *Journal for Preachers* 4,3 (Easter 1981): 13–17.

Childs, Brevard. *Biblical Theology in Crisis*. Philadelphia: Westminster Press, 1970.

Clowney, Edmund P. *Preaching and Biblical Theology*. Grand Rapids: Wm. B. Eerdmans, 1961.

Gowan, Donald E. *Reclaiming the Old Testament for the Christian Pulpit*. Atlanta: John Knox Press, 1980.

Harrington, Wilfrid J. *The Path of Biblical Theology*. Dublin: Gill and Macmillan, 1973: 349–403.

Keck, Leander E. *The Bible in the Pulpit*. Nashville: Abingdon Press, 1978: 69–99.

McKnight, Edgar V. *What Is Form Criticism?* Philadelphia: Fortress Press, 1969.

Miller, Donald G. *The Way to Biblical Preaching*. Nashville: Abingdon Press, 1957: 53–75.

Perrin, Norman. *What Is Redaction Criticism?* Philadelphia: Fortress Press, 1969.

Sloyan, Gerard F. "The Lectionary as a Context for Interpretation," *Interpretation* 31,2 (April 1977): 131–38.

Wedel, Theodore O. *The Pulpit Rediscovers Theology*. New York: Seabury Press, 1956: 63–105.

FOUR

Doctrine in Sacrament, Season, and Creed

If it is heresy to talk of preaching that does not start with a text, then heresy abounds. Listen to Henry Sloane Coffin: "We would not make it a hard and fast rule that a sermon must commence with a text. For variety's sake, it is well to preach occasionally without one. . . ."[1] Protestants may have traditionally started with a text and Roman Catholics with a doctrine, but the tables have turned this century—especially with the renewed interest in the Bible among Catholics since Vatican II and the continued interest in topical preaching among Protestants since Fosdick.

"For variety's sake" may sound like a weak reason to begin anywhere but the biblical text to preach a doctrinal sermon—or any kind of sermon, for that matter. I still believe, however, that the text is the best place to begin most of the time. Yet, like Coffin and countless other preachers, I do not believe that it is the only place to begin.

I have argued that in Christian preaching we indirectly preach doctrine all of the time. There is a theological perspective and theme underlying every sermon whether we begin with a text or not. The purpose of this chapter is to examine ways to preach doctrine directly by beginning consciously and unashamedly with a doctrine in sacrament, season, and creed.

Why do we preach with doctrine as a starting point? (1) Because the sacraments need explanation if we as Christians are to live in response to the grace that we receive from them. (2) Because the seasons of the church year are informed by doctrines that tell us of Christ, and they do this beyond the limitations of specific biblical texts. (3) Because the doctrines that comprise our creeds and confessions of faith demand preaching that can only

59

be done by direct treatment in series or single occasional sermons.

Using Brunner's categories, we come now to the second source of dogmatics—the *catechetical* element. There is not a great preacher in the history of the Christian pulpit who has not seen the importance of teaching through the sermon. Some have emphasized it more than others. Augustine believed teaching, or catechetics, to be the primary role of preaching. Preaching is to teach Christianity; the purpose of preaching is to instruct the believer—almost Calvin's words exactly. The preacher is the propagandist of the faith. The aims of any orator, Augustine believed (following Cicero), may be to teach, to touch, and to move, but the most important is to teach.

If believers do not know what they believe, how can they live the Christian faith? Inspirational sermons only go so far. A steady diet of heat with no light leads only to a heart strangely warmed and to a sad spiritual blindness. Christians must be pushed to think, to grow, to learn—to move beyond milk to solid food. Lyman Beecher was right when he told future preachers to write sermons that taxed their intellect and the intellect of their hearers.

There are many who have left our churches or gone elsewhere because our sermons did not teach doctrine or demand attention. They left because they learned nothing about Christianity and how to live it. Henry Sloane Coffin's nephew, William Sloane Coffin, has argued that people have not left the church because they have tried it and found it wanting, but because they have tried it and found it difficult. I believe he is wrong. Too many have not found the church difficult enough. I know that William Sloane Coffin is referring to the difficulty that accompanies social responsibility in the world, but Christians must be helped to see who they are in order for them to see how they should act in the world.

I am not talking about doctrinal sermons that are difficult because they are dull or too intellectual and unrelated to people's lives. Good, difficult doctrinal preaching teaches the meaning of the atonement or the incarnation by stretching the mind, the sinews of the faith, and opening new vistas for Christian experience. Good, difficult doctrinal preaching encourages the believer to ponder in depth the great doctrines of the faith.

Sometimes doctrinal preaching does so by introducing a *polemical* element. This is what Augustine did. The bulk of his sermons are set in the context of attacks on heresy. Often the best doctrinal preaching refines and purifies so that the hearers can tell the difference between fool's gold and the real thing. For Augustine, it meant calling a Donatist a Donatist or a Pelagian a Pelagian. For Calvin, it meant attacks on works-righteousness papists and man-centered libertines. For us, the clarifying may be to assist congregations in distinguishing between helpful, corrective criticism and unhealthy criticism of the present-day charismatic movement as we preach on the doctrine of the Holy Spirit. The purpose is never to create homiletical heresy hunts, but to get closer and closer to the truth about Jesus Christ as revealed in Scripture and brought to deeper understanding through our creeds and confessions.

Six Steps

The procedure for preaching with doctrine as the starting point is different from the one used when we began with a text. The process is much more complicated, although there are fewer rules. Doctrinal preaching of this sort involves much more homework. Following these steps will insure no shortcuts, but will help us keep our work focused.

1. We determine the biblical basis for this doctrine. We start here because of our belief that doctrinal preaching should be grounded in Scripture. Like the dogmatic theologian, we start with a complete, well-developed doctrine—sin, for example—and look back at Scripture to understand its roots, to determine whence it came. This is no simple task, for a doctrine like sin has made its way through centuries of thought and revision. Not only that, it permeates Scripture. Where do we start? Shall we talk of Adam and Eve and their fall from grace? How about David and Bathsheba? Will it be Israel's continual sin of idolatry which brought prophet after prophet into God's service? Perhaps it will be John the Baptist, exhorting all to repent, or Paul, insisting that we all "fall short." Sooner or later we realize that each part of the picture is not complete in itself. How do we get closer to the whole biblical picture of sin? Perhaps we should not. If we used all of the biblical picture, the sermon would last two weeks.

Yet I believe that we should attempt in our homework to get a holistic picture of the biblical view of sin. How else can we decide which direction the sermon should go? One way to do this is to check the concordance, looking up passages listed under "sin." A much quicker and often more helpful approach is to look up "sin" in the *Interpreter's Dictionary of the Bible* or a book like Alan Richardson's *A Theological Wordbook of the Bible*. Here you can get the big, overall picture. This larger picture does not blur distinctions, but brings them into sharper focus. From this vantage point, we can begin to see how sin has made its way from Eden to Easter and on toward the eschaton.

Since we cannot preach the whole Bible, we should settle in on one or two texts. This is not always necessary; there are occasions when a large doctrine goes beyond the scope of a single text. Charles Haddon Spurgeon often ranged around within the canon in his preaching with no single text. But as a rule, this is difficult to do successfully. The preacher serves up more than the congregation can handle at one sitting.

When deciding on one or two texts, we should do so fully aware of our hermeneutical decision-making process. For example, some of us may tend to think of sin as specific acts of wrongdoing. In order to downplay the idea that sin is indicative of the human predicament, we select our text from the first epistle of John and become almost Unitarian in our views. Others of us may go straight to Paul to show that sin is demonstrably universal, but that we are forgiven by God. However, reading Paul in a limited way can deemphasize the specific acts and the importance of living a holy life in response to God's grace, and can lead people into an "anything goes" attitude. Still others may overlook the corporate expression of sin in the Psalms and the prophets and center so much on the individual that the church never has anything to say to the world. Each of us, therefore, must examine our own hermeneutical decision-making process. Actually, it is good that theological perspective and personal preference influence our choice of texts when we begin to preach a doctrine. The variety of approaches adds richness and texture to Christian preaching, as long as we go into the process with our eyes open.

2. *We examine what major theologians have to say about the doctrine.* Once we have settled on a text or two (I say "two" since the doctrinal sermon may emerge from the conscious blending of two texts), we move to the thought of major theologians on the doctrine in question. We should determine which theologians—Calvin, Barth, Tillich, Rahner, etc.—we are going to read, then we should check the indexes of their works for the doctrine. (Luther is difficult to check, since he has no systematic theology.) We should steep ourselves in the theologians' words, focusing on how they apply to the texts we have selected. This will help in narrowing our reading since, especially with "sin," each has written a great deal. But as with Scripture, it never hurts to skim their broad assessments of the issues involved in the doctrine. From such a general reading, we might find a text that comes closer to the way we want to deal with "sin."

One approach that I have found helpful is to read both a theologian's dogmatic and biblical theology. For example, I not only read Calvin's *Institutes* on "sin," but I look at his *Commentaries* on the text or texts in question as well. Calvin always presents theological exegesis; however, in his *Institutes* he works as a dogmatic theologian looking back, while in his *Commentaries* he is a biblical theologian looking forward. Luther combines dogmatic and biblical theology in his writings.

Another, quicker, approach is to look up the doctrine in Alan Richardson's *A Dictionary of Christian Theology.* (Here "sin" is listed under the doctrine of man.) Richardson often offers a short history of Christian thought on the doctrines in question, talks a little about different theologians' perspectives, and in short order gives the big picture. Van A. Harvey's *A Handbook of Theological Terms* does the same thing much more briefly. A more thorough analysis comes with Rahner's *Encyclopedia of Theology,* which Roman Catholics will know and Protestants should know.

The importance of reading theologians is twofold. (1) It enables us to see how the doctrine has developed as it has progressed from biblical drama to theological dogma. (2) It helps us understand the doctrine clearly for ourselves. I believe Blackwood was right when he said, "Preach what you understand."[2] How can we expect our hearers to grasp the meaning of a doctrine if we do not understand it ourselves? Of course, some doctrines we will never understand fully. There is great mystery to all of them, and so there should be. But it is our responsibility to be clear about what we can know and what is beyond our knowledge and experience.

3. *We explore the images and experiences that relate to this doctrine.* The biblical images are numerous and readily available for the doctrine of sin. Here is Adam taking the first bite of the forbidden fruit, seeking to know more than he should, to be like God. There is Jacob at the Jabbok, finally having to face up to all his cheating and conniving. There is that Old Testament word *ḥāṭā* and that New Testament word *hamartanō* lurking throughout the canon, showing us how, like poor archers, we have "missed the mark," how, like pilgrims, we have gotten off the right road. Perhaps it is Peter saying three times, "Never met the man," or Pilate, like Lady Macbeth, washing, washing, "out, damned spot!"

The fact is that we cannot get rid of the spot. We know that; we have known it all along. The experience is deep. We see it in literature and in our lives, from Jean-Baptiste Clemence in Albert Camus's *The Fall* to the tragic Captain Ahab in Herman Melville's *Moby Dick*; from Nathaniel Hawthorne's Hester Prynne in *The Scarlet Letter* to Karl Shapiro's *Adam and Eve*, we see ourselves reflected in the tragic sin that all humanity has enjoyed and endured. Listen to William Shakespeare's Richard II:

> Though some of you with Pilate wash your hands,
> Showing an outward pity; yet you Pilates
> Have here delivered me to my sour cross
> And water cannot wash away your sins.[3]

Bruce Robertson (see his sermon in the appendix) changes the image from hand washing to mirror gazing. "St. Paul hands us a mirror. What depths are opened as we look into it: terror can be let loose by mirror gazing; vicious self-recrimination can be uncapped, fatigue and finitude are traced in the mirror, loneliness and the process of disease." We want to look away, but in the mirror of the biblical text we see ourselves for what we are—sinful. Do we need the images in literature to understand this doctrine? Perhaps not. It is so very real without them, more than any other doctrine. And yet they help us name the experience more specifically.

4. We examine the issues and problems that relate to this doctrine today. What are the heresies afoot with the doctrine of sin? Where can we help people grow in their Christian experience? Here are two entry points for dealing with this part of the homiletical procedure. The heresies are easy to identify. We do not even need to read Karl Menninger's *Whatever Became of Sin?* We see them in the "You're number one" books that fill the racks—nineteenth-century liberal humanism that sees us getting better and better. "Just think more positively about yourself, and everything will be wonderful." What a beautiful, Ebionite Christology! I wonder how many Unitarians there are in Christian churches these days. At least Unitarians believe that our acts have consequences. "Doing your own thing" can mean at some point treading on someone else's space.

At the other extreme, some see sin as so deep and pervasive that they never seem to believe God has forgiven them. The television evangelist Kenneth Copeland once told of a woman who came forward with eyes shut and arms uplifted, moaning about her sins and how awful her life was. When he talked with her and told her God had forgiven her in Christ, she continued to moan, despite his repeated assurances. Finally he slapped her and said, "Lady, you are forgiven!" Like those who still enjoy the adolescent conversion experience and never get beyond the first part of Fowler's stage three, this woman was enjoying getting high on the experience of lamenting her own sin.

Or, like the woman in Fowler's stage two, sin and salvation may be perceived as something that is kept in heaven. By saying her "Our Fathers" and "Hail, Marys" every day, she is able to store up enough grace in the bank to overcome the sin she has committed.[4] This concrete view of sin and salvation mixed with magic demonstrates a lack of understanding that may or may not be helped by sound preaching of Christian doctrine. But the growth cannot begin without specific attempts to deal with it from the pulpit.

For those who see sin only in individual terms, a doctrinal sermon on sin and evil in apocalyptic literature is in order. Read Revelation and Daniel; try to find individual sin there. You will not find it. Apocalyptic literature takes corporate evil seriously; so should we.

5. *We will focus our thought in one direction by establishing a central, clear purpose and staying with it.* This does not mean that the sermon can be summarized in one sentence. That rule is always difficult to keep. Focusing our thought in one direction is not quite so restricting. We should know clearly what we want to do with the sermon, and we should move throughout the sermon to that end. The purpose is determined by an analysis of the doctrine, its place in Scripture and tradition, and the needs of the congregation. Anything that does not fit that purpose is discarded or laid aside for another sermon. Our purpose may be to confront the congregation with the meaning of sin as disobedience and the wonder of God's grace despite our recalcitrance. This might come in a sermon that has the Ten Commandments as a text. If that is our purpose, then an extended excursus on original sin has no place in the sermon. Keep it taut. Stay with the purpose.

6. *Our structure will reflect allegiance to that purpose and the theological dimensions of the doctrine we have chosen to preach.* Here balance is very important, especially with the doctrine of sin. Even in a sermon on sin, it is appropriate to deal also with God's grace. Not to do so would be like singing only the first verse of Luther's *"Eine Feste Burg"* and leaving Satan in power—"With dread craft and might he arms himself to fight. On earth he has no equal." The question becomes how to deal with sin and how much space to give it. Certainly a doctrinal sermon on sin will seek to deal with it specifically, but how extensively?

Pastoral theologians offer helpful advice at this point. From hours of listening to people in pain, they realize that people come to church knowing of their sin, and at church they become aware of its depths. We preachers, they argue, do not need to drag our hearers through a description of sin at great length. We need instead merely to name and acknowledge it, then focus on helping people come to terms with it in light of God's grace.

But we do need to name sin for what it is. Not to do so would be an even more serious mistake. For there are not only Isaiahs in the temple saying, "Woe is me, for I am a man of unclean lips," fully aware of their own sin, but there are also Davids with Uriah's blood on their hands, who need a Nathan to say "Thou art the man!" William Oglesby sees this encounter clearly in pastoral counseling.

> The basic question of Genesis 3, "Where are you" (verse 9), fulfilled in him who came "to seek and save that which was lost" (Luke 19:10) is the key to the encounter. The essence of the encounter is the bringing together of truth and grace (John 1:17). Truth in this sense signifies a realistic affirmation of self, a "Here I am," together with a realistic understanding of the person, a "There you are," neither of which glosses over the harsh realities. Grace, by the same token, signifies the manifestation of forgiveness, the "I love you" which is real quite apart from any lovableness on the part of either. Without the word of truth, the word of grace is irrelevant; and without the word of grace, the word of truth is destructive.[5]

The parishioner comes with the consciousness of his or her own sin, the "Here I am," and the preacher must not pass by it as if it were unimportant. The preacher must say in effect, "Yes, there you are; you have sinned." Even if the parishioner comes with no sense of sin, the statement still holds. But as Oglesby points out, we also need the word of grace.

In this case, the structure of the doctrinal sermon is determined in part by the theological dimensions of the doctrine of sin and the ways in which it affects the believer. One could again choose from the variety of approaches listed in chapter 3, but the likelihood of employing the Barth, Calvin, or Edwards systems is diminished by the fact that we have not started with a specific text. If a passage happens to work this way, so much the better, but a point system or dialogical system will probably serve us more effectively, since they offer more freedom of structural expression.

With doctrine as our starting point, we turn now to the catechetical and polemical elements of doctrinal preaching by looking at sacrament, season, and creed and the challenges of the Lutheran law-gospel motif in doctrinal preaching.

Preaching the Sacraments

One of the best ways to teach doctrine in the pulpit is to preach about the sacraments on those days when they are celebrated. An infant has been baptized, the parents have held her up, as grace will hold her up throughout her life, and promised "to rear her in the nurture and the admonition of the Lord." An adult has come forward, having now committed his life to Christ and been baptized, initiated into Christ's kingdom. The table is set with the bread and the cup. There is a moment of expectation. The people are ready to partake of the sacrament—to eat, drink, and remember.

Now is the time for us to preach on the sacraments. We should do such preaching directly, particularly with baptism. Those in the Anglo-Catholic traditions and in the Disciples of Christ church who celebrate the Eucharist weekly do not always feel the constraint to make connections each time they preach. For them the visual symbol is present regularly. But even these traditions find it necessary on occasion to teach the doctrine of the Eucharist so that parishioners will partake with understanding.

The number of parishioners in our time who know little or nothing about the sacraments is startling. What they do know is even more startling, for in many cases it borders on the heretical and the magical. Think of Archie Bunker of "All in the Family," who, concerned over little Joey's mortal soul, slipped out of the house with the child, taking him to a local church for baptism.

Archie tried to enlist the aid of a minister, but the young minister was unable to oblige. So Archie tried to convince him with a five-dollar bill. When that did not work, Archie went to the baptistry and, in a touching moment, baptized the little fellow himself.

Imagine if Archie had heard a sermon that helped him see that baptism is the sacrament of initiation into the Christian community—an act that communicates the power and love of God as the child is now placed in God's hand and takes Christ's hand in his daily walk in faith. Archie is unfortunately still in Fowler's stages one and two, where religion is seen in magical terms. Some good straight doctrinal preaching on the meaning of baptism might help move him ahead in his Christian pilgrimage. But who can tell with Archie?

There are, of course, many "Archies" in our churches today. They come when they want; they live on a Sunday-school faith, if even that. C. Ellis Nelson puts it this way:

> Normally, the child at confirmation receives a theologically correct definition of the traditional belief about worship and the sacraments, and there the matter lies for the rest of his life. Unless the child is unusually inquisitive, he gets no further instruction except what may come incidentally in communion sermons. His mind is religiously arrested at the teenage level.[6]

Our responsibility as preachers is to challenge the teenage minds of our adults—to move them to a deeper faith by opening for them the doctrinal meaning of the sacraments according to their biblical roots.

This task is both catechetical and polemical. We teach that baptism is our initiation into the body of Christ, our being ingrafted into Christ through the outpouring of the Holy Spirit. We also correct false understandings. For example, baptism is primarily God's action, not ours. If we can see it that way, then we will put less emphasis on the specific mode of baptism, for it is not so much what *we* do but what *God* has done in Christ, and it is God's doing through the Spirit that really counts. Likewise, to turn the service into a social occasion—a kind of theological debut for the baby, a spiritual coming out—again places too much emphasis on human action.

In preaching on the sacraments, it is not always necessary to speak from a specific text, but it is necessary to understand the different biblical perspectives and how they offer different angles on the meaning of baptism. For example, if we only read Acts 2, where many consciously repented and were baptized, and Romans 6, where Paul talks of "dying and rising with Christ," one could preach pretty vehemently for only adult believers' baptism (which is more easily defended by Scripture alone anyway). But when the subject is the Holy Spirit's descending on Christ and the fact that we are "all sons and daughters of God" (Galatians 3), the emphasis is more on God's action than on our repentance in turning toward Christ. This is one reason why Presbyterians, among others, support both practices. Those who follow believers' baptism alone tend to place less emphasis on God's prior action and grace in the sacrament and more emphasis on the action of the believer.

Those who allow for baptism of infants do so with a stronger emphasis on God's prevenient grace. To understand God's love and grace, think of parents who really love their children, who spend time with them. These parents have a love for their children that is independent from the children's subjective responses or changing moods. When they first brought their infants home from the hospital, they already had much love for them. They love them through the terrible twos and the giggling fours, through broken windows and smart-alecky back talk. They love them as recalcitrant adolescents and as rebellious young adults. God's love for us is also like this, for it is independent of our response. It is not governed by our poor show of love for God. Instead it is given freely, for we have been adopted into God's family as children who were lost but now have been found. God takes us—homeless, nameless, forgotten, ready to be tossed to the world. And God adopts us before we know any better, and cares for us throughout our lives, watching over us even when we turn away. God never gives up on us. Therefore, baptism is not our human action, but God's action in Christ Jesus our Lord.

The Lord's Supper is also God's action on our behalf in Christ. It is Christ's sacrifice for us, his body broken and his blood spilled on our behalf. Our action is simply to receive in faith and to "do this in remembrance" of him—to let our actions be loving ones, empowered by his Spirit in this sacrament and done in his name.

"Real presence" used to be fighting words in the church. For some they may still be, although we now live in a post-Enlightenment, post-Kantian era. It is difficult to make sense of the Aristotelian meanings of "accidents" and "substance," for we do not think in these categories anymore. We are the heirs of the nominalist philosophy. We believe that "a rose is a rose is a rose," and not something else. We are not heirs of the Fourth Lateran Council, which in 1215 solidified the idea of transubstantiation and which spent so much time debating the way Christ was present in the Sacrament that the power and the mystery of the message was missed.

On the other hand, many today, both Catholic and Protestant, have followed Ulrich Zwingli and turned the Eucharist into a "mere memorial." They have done this not so much because of Zwingli—most have never heard of him—but because empiricism is the mark of our age. We know what we can see and touch and smell. Those Protestants who follow Calvin's dynamic virtualism (Christ present in power), and those Roman Catholics who follow Odo Casel's transsignification (which talks of Christ's presence, but not spatially)[7] offer a deeper understanding of the meaning of Christ's presence in the Lord's Supper. For them, Christ's presence is the work of the Holy Spirit as the power and forgiveness of Christ is made present in the hearts of the believers. Their emphasis is not only on Christ's passion and atonement but on his incarnation as a whole. Christ's teaching and healing ministries are seen here. Christ is the "Word made flesh," who dwelt among us, the one who "emptied himself" and who is exalted at the right hand of the throne of God. All this comes to a point as we celebrate Holy Communion.

But we cannot preach it all in one doctrinal sermon. Thus, as with baptism and other doctrines, we attempt only partial views of the glorious mystery. One helpful way to do this is to examine

the eucharistic service itself. What does it mean that we are all
called together to share the feast which God has prepared? Is this
the fellowship symbolized in the sacrament itself, sitting at the
Great Supper of the Lamb? Look at the Great Thanksgiving, the
eucharistic prayer. What is the meaning of the anamnesis? How
are we to remember Christ? Why pray the epiclesis? What does it
mean to call upon the Holy Spirit? Here are great teaching opportunities.

In a sermon given during Advent one year, I took the phrase
from the words of the institution, "You proclaim the Lord's
death until he comes," (1 Cor. 11:26) and preached it with a
Barthian-type structure. We were celebrating Holy Communion,
so the sermon pointed not only to the table but to the coming of
the Christ child. "You proclaim the Lord's death" became the
first point on which I spoke. What an odd thing to focus on right
before Christmas! Advent is not a time for sadness or remorse; it
is a time for joy, for celebration. But if Christ is not seen as
headed for Calvary, then he is just another child in a manger.
Even the fourth verse of that popular Christmas hymn, "We
Three Kings of Orient Are," speaks of Christ's death. So perhaps
even at Christmastime we should proclaim the Lord's death.

For the second point, I focused on the rest of the phrase: "until
he comes." Advent is a time of waiting, waiting for the Coming
One who has come once but who will come again. Here the
second coming motif of Advent appears. I thus preached a doctrinal sermon that led to Holy Communion, using for my text words
that were said over bread and wine, and I also brought to bear on
the Eucharist two other doctrinal themes as well.

There is something powerful about the Lord's Supper which
needs to be conveyed when we preach about it. Perhaps its power
lies in the command "This do in remembrance of me." Those
words, which we see etched on the front of so many altars and
communion tables, are Christ's words. They speak to us through
the centuries, as meaningful now as they have been in the past.

A few years ago I met with military personnel in Berchtesga-
den, West Germany. We were gathered there from all over West-

ern Europe—and even as far away as Turkey—officers and enlisted men from all the services and some British soldiers as well. On the last night of our retreat, we gathered to celebrate the Lord's Supper. We met in the hotel where Joseph Goebbels and Hermann Goering used to stay when Adolf Hitler brought his high command together to plan various offenses. Outside the window, the Alps stood, reaching up into the twilight. It was an electric moment. Two words—*"Heil Hitler!"*—once echoed through those halls, two words that once bloodied the face of Europe. But they could be heard no longer. They had been replaced by other words that night—older words, words with even more power: "This do in remembrance of me."

When we preach the sacraments, we preach the power of God; we preach Christ and Christ crucified. When we preach the sacraments to teach and to correct, we should do so with vigor and joy and enthusiasm, trusting in the power of the Holy Spirit.

Preaching the Christian Year

In addition to preaching the sacraments, we also teach and correct by preaching the seasons of the church year. Most of Christendom regularly observes the church year calendar; why not preach the doctrines that inform it? In chapter 3, we discussed how the passages in the lectionary are chosen for the most part to correspond with certain theological themes. When we preach doctrinally by beginning with the lectionary, we operate like biblical theologians who start with a text and then attempt to discover the doctrines that have their roots in Scripture. We are bound to confront more doctrines if we follow this process, that is, starting with a text, since not all the epistle lessons are chosen to accommodate the overarching theological schemes for various seasons. When we begin with the church year itself—Advent, Christmas, Epiphany, Easter, and Pentecost—to determine the theological themes, the process is reversed.

I once asked a seminary class to create a one-year lectionary. First they had to examine ten or twelve lectionaries from around the world to see how they were put together. With each one, they tried to understand the hermeneutical and theological presuppositions of the various committees that composed them. After examining several lectionaries, one finds it easier to see the hermeneutic working behind the choice of texts. For example, the older United Presbyterian lectionary for the *Service for the Lord's Day* was highly Trinitarian. It was divided into three sections: (1) God the Son—from Advent to Ascension; (2) God the Holy Spirit—from Pentecost to the nineteenth Sunday after Pentecost; and (3) God the Father—the last eight weeks before Advent. The older United Methodist lectionary put Kingdomtide toward the end of Pentecost to give an earlier introduction to the eschatological thrust that would come in Advent. While studying these lectionaries, the students discovered the various doctrines that seem to emerge as crucial with each season. Once they had discovered which doctrines were central to each season, they were able to choose passages to fit the doctrines. This, then, is the process of the dogmatic theologian who looks back to Scripture to find supporting texts.

What are some of these crucial theological themes? *Advent* begins the church year by announcing the coming of the king—the Christ Child. As we noted before, however, the coming refers also to Christ's second coming—where Christ is not only king, but judge. Thus we presently live in the time between the times—the already-but-not-yet. We wait expectantly—hence the use of apocalyptic passages during Advent. But our waiting is not entirely passive, despite the fact that apocalyptic literature calls for passive resistance of evil. We are to repent. No wonder John the Baptist is so popular during Advent. The Baptist, and behind him the whole Old Testament, point to Christ; specifically, they point to the hope we have in Christ. That hope is strongly expressed: no matter what happens, no matter what kind of destruction humankind brings upon itself, God will have the last word. The gates of hell shall not prevail against the church. In a nuclear age, that is an especially powerful word.

Advent points to *Christmas*, one of those questionable holidays in the Christian year. Historically, Christmas is associated with the pagan Roman winter solstice, the birth of the Unconquered

Sun, celebrated on December 25. Not knowing Jesus' actual birthday, the church put Christmas in the place of this Roman holiday. Calvinists in Scotland abolished Christmas Day, and some still see it as only a secular experience, even in this country. Nevertheless, we celebrate it in the church today. Its main theological theme is obvious—the incarnation of Christ. What must be made very clear in doctrinal preaching during this season is that we preach not only the birth of a babe but the birth of the King of kings, who lived our life, who died as we do, who rose as victor over death. Christmas is not limited to a manger. John Donne writes:

> The whole life of Christ was a continual passion; others die Martyrs, but Christ was born a martyr. He found a Golgotha even in Bethlehem, for, to his tenderness then, the strawes are almost as sharp as the thornes after; and the Manger as uneasie at first, as his Crosse at last. His birth and his death were but one continual act, and his Christmas Day and his Good Friday are but the evening and the morning of one and the same day.[8]

Donne does not overstate the point. During Christmas we preach incarnation to mean life, death, and resurrection.

Epiphany is full of doctrines. Christ is revealed in all his glory. This manifestation and revelation of God come through Christ's baptism and through his transfiguration. Dark and light images flicker on the stage of this divine drama mixed with dogma. We catch glimpses of Christ's glory in the mission to the Gentiles— the message is to be carried to all who will hear it. But divine power is unleashed here as well. God is sovereign over all nature and history. The very stars point to Christ's birth. Kings bow down to him. Some even tremble before him, for Herod is powerless to prevent his coming into the world; countless Herods have failed to stamp out his name or halt the onward march of his church. Here is doctrine that will preach!

Lent repeats the theme of repentance already introduced in Advent, as the catechumens prepare for baptism and joining the church. This season is a time of testing, of temptation, which leads to and includes *Palm Sunday,* where the theme of Christ's kingship is mixed with Christ's passion. As Christ enters Jerusa-

lem, he heads toward the Last Supper, Eucharist, and the cross—
the atonement. Atonement is one of the hardest doctrines to
preach. The problem certainly is not finding an image; there is no
shortage of images. We have the sacrificial image in Hebrews,
where Christ is both high priest and the perfect sacrifice; there is
the exemplarist image of Abelard, where Christ is merely a
model—the supreme example of a suffering servant. We cannot
overlook Anselm's legal, or juridical, image which, like the courtroom scenes of Paul's thoughts in Rom. 5:6–11, as well as in 2
Cor. 5:16–21, talks of God's satisfaction, yet, unlike Paul, does
not show God taking the initiative, but only being paid off through
Christ's death. We also confront the battlefield imagery of Gustav
Aulen's *Christus Victor*, where Christ defeats Satan in the divine
drama. Finally, the financial image of slaves' ransom being paid
by one man comes through 1 Cor. 6:20 and 7:23, and 1 Pet. 1:18–
19.

Get behind these images to the experiences to which they
point. See the empty heart of the world, lonely and broken, sepa-
rated from its Maker, fearing death and, even more, life itself.
Look at the proud, and those seeking satisfaction in their own
success, but never quite getting enough. It is all there behind the
cross. Christ took it all upon himself—that fear of death, that
suffering, that self-centeredness—and in one great act of love,
demonstrated the love of our God. As Stewart puts it, "The veil
had been hanging there for years, but on that night it was rent
from top to bottom for all to see God's love."[9] Read Gary Jen-
nings's book *Aztec* to catch the contrast vividly. Our God is not
one who must be appeased by daily human sacrifices. The blood
of God's own Son was spilled for us. What kind of a God is this?
One unlike any other in the history of religions. Stewart is right—
there is a startling paradox to the atonement. It is more than a
theory. It is sheer love that contradicts all reason—a scandal to
Jews and just plain foolishness to Greeks. The wonder of it—a
God so meek that he would stoop to save you and me! That is the
richness of the atonement, and it demands to be preached. Therefore, we should preach the cross knowing the theories, avoiding
the heresies, and bringing the images into contact with daily life.

Easter, the first day and the oldest season of the Christian year, is the pinnacle of the Christian experience. There is at least one seminary professor who refuses to send Christmas cards for this reason. Instead, he sends his annual Easter epistle. We should reorder our thinking, he argues, and return to the church's earliest roots—the celebration of the resurrection. Whether or not to send Easter cards is one question, but whether to preach the resurrection—there is no question about that.

This season rounds out the three great actions of Christ's work. Through the Christmas/Epiphany cycle, we hear of the incarnation. In Lent and Holy Week we study the atonement, but at Easter our goal is to preach the resurrection—no easy task. As David Buttrick points out, the Easter message is an incredible story, that is, it is literally hard to believe. The reason we find the resurrection—and the sacraments—difficult to believe is that we are such a secular people. Buttrick finds secularism the mark of our age.

> What doubles difficulty on Easter is our current secularism. . . . Nowadays we are *all* secular people, preachers included. While we may be a secular people who affirm Jesus Christ, our style is still decidedly secular. . . . If medieval man saw a cross by the roadside, he may have thought of the cross on which his Savior died; we speed past a cross near a superhighway and guess that someone is advertising a church.[10]

Buttrick is right. This is a difficult day for preachers who have a lifetime of Easter days on which to preach to their biggest crowds. Year in, year out, the message is the same. Listen to one such message:

> I have a confession to make to you. For years, on Easter day, a little voice somewhere inside of me has said, "This is all make-believe. It isn't real. You are pretending to something you don't really believe." The same voice has often raised itself at funerals. "It's nice to pretend that there is life after death, but you can't really believe it."[11]

As it turns out, this "confession" made a great entry into a sermon on the doubt and fear of the women who fled from Jesus' tomb at the odd conclusion of Mark's Gospel (16:1–8). But there is also a sense in which the minister was being honest and perhaps speaking what many clergy have felt. We may wonder how to preach the resurrection even when we strongly believe it. If we do not believe in the resurrection, Paul informs us in 1 Cor. 15:12–16 that the whole Christian faith topples like a deck of stacked cards. The resurrection is the one card that counts.

What are the problems connected with preaching the resurrection?

1. Most Christians do not have difficulty with the basic Christian kerygma in Paul's letters. The difficulty comes with the apparent contradiction of the resurrection narratives in the Gospels. This point made by Joseph Fitzmyer is well taken: How do you reconcile Mark's abrupt ending with the numerous appearances of the risen Christ in the other three Gospels?[12]

2. Another problem is the way we view Christ's "risenness" as it is depicted in the various accounts. Fitzmyer suggests that a close reading of the text will make clear that "the New Testament never presents the resurrection of Jesus as a resuscitation, i.e., a return to his former mode of terrestrial existence," like Lazarus, for example. When Christ appears, it is "in glory," but as a "glorified body," not some mystical ghost. Thus Fitzmyer believes that the New Testament supports a bodily resurrection, not in the Greek but in the "Palestinian Jewish Christian" sense.[13] I believe Merrill Abbey is correct in suggesting that debating about the form of Christ's resurrection from the pulpit can prove counterproductive. But meeting the issue head-on can be helpful, especially if your ultimate goal is not to argue a theory but to help people meet their risen Lord.[14]

3. Buttrick believes that too many people wrongly assume that the resurrection points to our immortality. The reason for this assumption is their failure to take death seriously.[15] Hence, responsible doctrinal preaching on the resurrection requires that we begin by helping people come to terms with death. Death is real and no respecter of persons. We do not somehow "slip by it" because we are Christians. Not even Christ "slipped by it." He suffered as we will, yet for our sakes.

When we preach the resurrection, then, we will not dodge the difficult issues posed by the New Testament. We will not mince words when we talk of death. We will clarify confidently and then speak boldly that just as God said at Christ's baptism, "This is the one," and inaugurated his ministry, so at his resurrection God validated Jesus' life and his lordship over the church and the world. By God's power Christ was raised, like the dead dry bones of Israel, and by God's power we, too, will be raised. We will remember with William Muehl the pathos of the resurrection event which steers us away from sentimentality. Easter is more than flowers budding and sap running as rites of spring. It goes deeper. From Good Friday to Easter, there is "victory in every defeat, and defeat in every victory." That is what we will preach. And we have seven Sundays to do this, since Easter is not one day but a whole season.

We preach the resurrection, moving toward ascension and Christ's exaltation to the right hand of God. If resurrection is foreign to our thoughts, ascension is even more so. Ascension is shrouded in a great cloud of mystery. It is the last manifestation of Christ to his disciples, but such an odd one. What is the theological point? Not that Jesus has power to fly like Superman; the ascension is not a spatial experience, despite the fact that it is framed that way. The cosmology of the first century no longer holds in an age of airplanes and astronauts.

The ascension shows that Christ has been received into the realm of God, that unseen world that we will someday experience and that we know is as real as the unseen world of truth, friendship, and love.[16] Christ's ascension does not mean that he has withdrawn further from us, but that he has brought us closer to the unseen world of God's presence. Ascension combines the immanence of God and the hope we have in Jesus Christ, who has gone into God's presence before us. We preach the ascension not as a doctrine of Christ's going away but as a doctrine of God drawing nearer to us.

With the very long season of *Pentecost,* we celebrate the coming of the Holy Spirit and the doctrine of the Trinity. The Holy Spirit is difficult to preach. Some preachers avoid the Spirit so much that they are almost "binitarian." Charismatics have at least encouraged us to take another look at the Spirit. The Holy Spirit is not an extra person in the Trinity but is the Spirit of Christ, the Spirit of God, the *ruach,* the *pneuma* which dwells in us and prompts our grateful worship. We cannot control the Spirit of Christ any more than we can control the wind, but we know when the Spirit has moved us. Sometimes you can almost see the Spirit coming; it is like sitting in a sailboat on a still day and waiting for the wind. As you sit passively in the boat, unable to sail, you see the wind coming on the water. When it comes close, you watch it fill your sails and you feel its movement. When the Holy Spirit comes close, it also creates movement. Preachers sometimes wonder why their hearers are so moved by a sermon that barely made it out of the study, much less off the ground. Perhaps it was the Spirit, they say. Like runners who have received their "second wind," perhaps the sermon has had breathed into it new meaning—a second wind—from the Spirit. Of course, the analogies and images used to describe the Spirit must be chosen very carefully in order to maintain scriptural and theological integrity.

This point is even more true when preaching the Trinity. Again, Donald Baillie is helpful.

> [T]he doctrine of the Trinity is not simply a doctrine of a divine trio, but a doctrine of *one* in three, of three persons, Father, Son, and Holy Spirit, in one God. *One God:* that is the starting point, the background.[17]

Baillie knows that trying to pin the Trinity to one text or to prove the Trinity from Scripture is risky business. But he believes that two completely new events occurred in history—two events that stand center stage in the New Testament to help us understand the Trinity. One was the life, death, and resurrection of Jesus Christ, which did not change the monotheism of the Jews, but added new meaning to it. The other was the undeniably magnificent scene at Pentecost, when the church was born. God was still one, but with richer, fuller meaning for those who worshiped God.[18]

The two other major theological themes in the season of Pentecost are the church, with all its attendant images—body of Christ, bride of Christ, holy nation, royal priesthood, God's own people—and sanctification, which in the process of salvation follows repentance and justification, doctrines covered in other seasons as well as this one. The overarching theme of this season, then, is Christian growth—the growth of the individual toward holiness and the growth of the church as the body of Christ into Christ who is the head—that rich vision of high Christology in Ephesians.

It should be obvious by now that we do not really preach the church year, but Christ, for every season points to him, to some aspect of his person and work. As with the sacraments, so with the Christian year, our main goal is to preach Christ in all his humility and in all his glory. When we preach the Christian year doctrinally, we are not merely preaching a set of doctrines, but the story of Christ. Those who talk of story in preaching are correct on this score.[19] We need to see our story in the context of the story of Christ. If we can learn to preach Christ with that in mind, the doctrines of the church year will come alive with new fervor and excitement.

It is obvious that following the lectionary will bring us into contact with the doctrines that inform the church year, but on occasion we should preach these doctrines directly, not feeling bound to the lectionary texts.

Confessional Homiletics

The move from church year to confession of faith is not a large one; the same doctrines of the Trinity—Father, Son, and Holy Spirit—and the work of each through creation and redemption in nature, history, the church, and the Christian life are found in both. Some confessions, like the Apostles' Creed, omit more refined but basic doctrines like repentance, justification, and sanctification. The oldest confession, "Jesus is Lord," omits a great deal. But it also tells us a lot. The utterance is more than an intellectual statement made in a vacuum. It is a deep, heartfelt expression of a believer, and yet a believer standing within a community where every knee is bowing and every tongue confessing Jesus as Lord.

But it goes deeper still. The genuflection is not only a religious posture, but the evidence of a political statement. In America, we bow to no one; we barely respect the president. In the time of Paul's letter to the Philippians, however, people did plenty of bowing. "Jesus is Lord" is thus a political statement. Following Christ means primary allegiance to him, and Caesar is second. Take it or leave it. "Jesus is Lord" may be limited in theological breadth, but not in christological depth. Not every confession offers the range of doctrines found in the church year, but when studied in their scriptural and ecclesiastical contexts, they do present a richness of theological insight.

A minister once told me of his experience in a Dutch Reformed church in New York City. He was required to preach through the entire Heidelberg Catechism every four years. Here the catechism served as a kind of doctrinal lectionary deeply rooted in Scripture and tradition. In the old Evangelical and Reformed church (now part of the United Church of Christ), preachers were encouraged but not required to preach from this creed. Is it not interesting that preachers within the Reformed tradition would begin preaching with anything but the biblical text? Not only that, they were required to do this.

There is some wisdom in this approach. The creeds have always offered the church a rich tradition of doctrinal expression. What exactly is the purpose of the creeds, and why should we preach them? The creeds tie us to our historical roots in the mighty deeds of God. We are more than a group of separate adherents, holding our own subjective beliefs; we are established in salvation history, not our own individual piety. The creeds put us in direct contact with our story, the biblical story of faith. Like a compass, they give us a guide through Scripture, help us to understand the biblical message, and correct our mistaken interpretations. Even in textual preaching, where we do not intend to preach doctrine explicitly, the creeds aid us in right thinking theologically. The creeds link us also to our origins in the church. We are not only twentieth-century Christians but believers whose roots go way back. Preaching the creeds gives us this historical perspective.

This grounding in the church also broadens our denominational base, for the creeds defy sectarianism; they move us beyond our own narrow ecclesial bounds into more universal, ecumenical ways of thinking about the faith. To be sure, each church has its creeds (except for some free churches). Creeds help draw the lines between the churches here and there. But all churches return to the great early creeds. The reformers who wanted to retain their ties to the one true catholic church appealed to the Apostles', Nicene, and Athanasian Creeds. Presbyterians still say at least the first of these from memory Sunday after Sunday. The Roman Catholic breviary still includes the Apostles' Creed as a unifying bond among Christian confessions. Thus we have used the creeds liturgically for years. They show us our roots and bring us together in worship and belief.

In addition to appearing liturgically with the sacraments in the baptismal rite and the Eucharist, the creeds have also been used polemically and catechetically. The former is no surprise, since many of the creeds arose in the heat of theological turmoil as responses to heresy within the church. We can also use them polemically in doctrinal preaching today, in a way that does not castigate or attack others, but clarifies and corrects mistaken ideas about the Christian faith.

There are those in the church who believe only in a sweet Jesus—a mystical, loving Spirit who never lived or died, but only floated about. Their Jesus never went into the ghetto or identified with the poor. He seemed never to get his hands dirty. Such modern-day Docetism is rampant in our churches. What shall we do? We shall preach to them the Christ of the creeds. He "suffered under Pontius Pilate, was crucified, dead, and buried. . . ." No floating Spirit would ever do that! Many churches avoid saying, "He descended into hell," because this carries the suffering too far. Listen to Jürgen Moltmann on this phrase in the creed:

> If we compare the faith in the Christ who descended into hell with the hell that makes our life on earth unbearable, then we find the courage to identify the crucified with those who suffer. Christ was not crucified between two candles on the altar, but between two exiles on a rocky hill outside the city. He has become the brother of the abandoned, the lonely, the tortured, the innocent who are mur-

dered and the guilty who are despised. He is on their side, not on the other. They may be in fear of hell, but they are not alone. God has left his high place and is present with his abandoned ones. Our God is there, in the disgrace, in the beaten, in those whose lives we have turned into hell. This means that we should not look to ourselves, fixed in the moment of our misery on earth. "Look to the wounds of Christ, for there has your hell been mastered" (Luther).[20]

Moltmann's words offer not only correction but comfort. Responsible polemical preaching is always theologically penetrating and pastorally sensitive.

Perhaps the hearers believe that Caesar is first and Christ second, that the church should remain under the control of the government. What shall we do? We shall preach the biblical message of *The Theological Declaration of Barmen,* which was born in the midst of Nazi occupation and which combined into a single voice the Lutheran, Reformed, and United churches. It is a creed grounded in Scripture and ready throughout to "reject the false doctrine" that the church should bow down to political ideology.

In the history of the early church, the catechetical use of the creeds appeared especially in the training of those who had not yet been baptized. For us today, this practice touches three audiences. (1) The first audience is comprised of adults in the church who are still children in the faith. Some are outsiders—resident aliens and tourists. Others are insiders—expatriates and cynical citizens. Whatever the case, their understanding of Christianity is childlike. They seem, oddly enough, to get more out of the children's message than the sermon. (2) The second group is made up of the young teenagers who are about ready to join the church, but who have little idea of the church's doctrine. The creeds become excellent resources for simple, catechetical preaching to both these teenagers and to the adults mentioned in the previous category. (3) The third group consists of children of kindergarten and early elementary school age, who are occasionally or weekly subjected to the children's sermon. Some are mercifully spared from this experience.

I mention the children's sermon at this point to introduce a bias and a possible historical solution to a real problem for many present-day clergy. There is nothing more ridiculous than seeing a robed figure squatting on a stool, trying to be cute and clever on Sunday morning. This figure is not the divine incarnation—God come down. Nor is this situation similar to Jesus and the children. That, after all, was no liturgy. The point of the New Testament account was that Jesus did not mind the interruption; he certainly did not stage it! But we cannot argue against children's sermons because some are so bad ("God is dog spelled backwards, and both are faithful"; "Jesus is like a jumper cable—he charges you up") or because they only present little morals like "Be good to your sister"—mere cultural pablum. By that line of reasoning, we would have to dispense with preaching as well, for not all Christian preaching is responsible or great.

I am not against a little humanness in the midst of the majesty of worship—the shuffle of little feet punctuating the holy hush. The problem with children's sermons is that they say to children implicitly, "You don't really belong here, so we are going to set aside this special time for you, and then you can leave." A seminary student once appeared at my door looking confused. "What will I do? I have to give three messages on Sunday." He showed me the bulletin. Sure enough, there they were: children's sermon, teen scene, and sermon. "What in the world is teen scene?" I asked. "Oh, that's when the fifteen- and sixteen-year-olds come forward to loiter in the chancel with their hands in their back pockets." What is next, I thought—elderly hour? Menopause meditation? We might as well bring the whole congregation forward in little groups.

Others have studied this problem more thoroughly than I, analyzing children with the help of Jean Piaget, Erik Erikson, Lawrence Kohlberg, James Fowler, and so on. With graphs and charts, they can tell you how much the little ones can understand at different ages. This is fine and helpful, but I believe that Horace Bushnell would be chuckling these days. He was right all along: bring them up so they do not know themselves to be anything but Christians. I believe he would have said, "Put them in the pew and let them worship as early as possible, at least by age five or six. Liturgy is not to be understood completely, anyway; it is to be experienced. Let them worship right along with their parents."

If we find that we must do children's sermons (because of the insistence of our church boards), then we should use the model of the early church in its catechesis for the unbaptized. In the liturgy of the catechumens, the unbaptized were instructed in the faith, usually in the creeds. Why not use the children's sermon in this way, and offer through it little teachings in the faith? On sacramental Sundays, invite the children to stand alongside the parents of the child to be baptized, or to come to the Table before the bread and wine are passed. Many are already employing this kind of approach.

The jump from a children's sermon in this fashion to a doctrinal sermon for the congregation is not very large, for both involve teaching doctrine from the creeds in as simple a manner as possible. How do we do that? First of all, by helping our hearers make distinctions between common beliefs and debatable interpretations. For example, in Christology we all agree that Christ is God's Son in whom God is manifest, and that he is Savior and Lord. We may not agree on the theories of his origin, the extent of his preexistence, the degree of his humanity and his divinity, or the correct way to explain his atoning death on the cross. Some aspects of Christology we agree on; others will find us fine tuning this way or that. Congregations need help sorting out common belief and interpretation. They need to hear the basics preached confidently. But they also need to know that there are many Christologies in the New Testament, not just one. They can handle redaction criticism as long as it is presented clearly and simply in the context of a teaching sermon, not an erudite lecture.

Second, we preach the creeds fully aware of their provisional character. The church is constantly reforming. No creed is the last word on Christian doctrine. All confessions are time bound. Theology, of necessity, must progress; it must move on. Barth understood that as well as anyone. He did not want little Barths, but serious theologians carrying the task forward. We will preach the creeds, keeping in mind that they are not the final word about

God and his people. This does not mean tentative preaching, but preaching that understands the provisional character of confessions of faith.

Third, we should attempt a series of sermons on a creed, either a short series—no more than six or eight weeks, lest our congregations wear down—or a much longer series like the Dutch Reformed do by using the Heidelberg Catechism. The longer series will take some agreement by the congregation. The Heidelberg Catechism, as we noted earlier, is already designed with fifty-two Sundays in mind, which creates for the preacher a theological lectionary.[21]

If the Scots Confession were used this way, it could follow this pattern. Chapter 1, God, could be used around Thanksgiving, since it deals with providence. The next four chapters work nicely with Advent: creation, original sin, promise, and the roll call of the cloud of witnesses looking to Christ. Chapters 6 and 7 are obvious for Christmas and Epiphany: the incarnation of Christ Jesus and why the Mediator had to be true God and true man. Chapter 8 on election puts more emphasis on God's action than our repentance, but could still be used in Lent. Chapters 9—11 are natural for Palm Sunday, Holy Week, and Easter: Christ's passion, death, and burial; the resurrection; and the ascension. Chapter 12, as you might have guessed, is faith in the Holy Ghost. The rest of the chapters work well with Pentecost, dealing variously with the church, the Christian life, the Scriptures, the sacraments, and church-state relations. The very last chapter would even give theological backbone to a stewardship sermon which would probably appear at about that time: gifts freely given to the church.

In 1528, Luther preached the Apostles' Creed as part of a series of sermons on the catechism. He did so for catechetical purposes. He believed that Christians should know what they believe or not be admitted to the Table. The editors of these sermons write, "It is apparent that Luther is here forming the vocabulary into which he cast both his Large and Small Catechisms, and that the Large Catechism is particularly a reworking of this catechetical preaching."[22] Luther understood the importance of preaching the creeds. Read the third sermon in the appendix to see how he preaches on the creed. Here he handles the whole creed in one sermon for a specific purpose.

Finally, we will preach the creeds remembering that there is a subjective side to them. The believers who first confessed these creeds did not do so as a stimulating intellectual exercise. Rather, they were committing their whole lives to Jesus Christ. When we preach these creeds, we are engaged in more than a didactic exercise. We are also preaching to the emotion and the will. Bonhoeffer, in his Finkenwald lectures, distinguishes between didactic, inspirational, and conversion sermons.[23] Each has a different purpose, he says, and in a larger sense, he is right. But I believe, as did Augustine, that good doctrinal preaching involves all three. It seeks to teach the mind, to touch the heart, and to move the will. For Augustine the most important purpose may have been to teach, but the final purpose was to lead Christians to live a holy life. The persuasion was not only to attitude, but to action: "As a hearer must be pleased in order to secure his attention, so he must be persuaded in order to move him to action. . . ." People can be taught and delighted without giving consent. What is "the use of gaining the first two, if we fail in the third?"[24]

A presidential candidate completes his or her speech. One of the hearers is interviewed. "What did you think?" "Wonderful speech—clever, witty, informational, patriotic—moved me to tears." "So you're going to vote for this candidate?" "No." A good doctrinal sermon teaches, touches, *and* moves the will. With Stewart, we believe that doctrinal preaching should move from doctrine to decision. We will preach the creeds knowing that doctrine begun in action must lead to action, that creed should lead to deed.

> Love so amazing, so divine
> Demands my soul, my life, my all.

Preaching Law and Gospel

The move from doctrine to decision points to some kind of call to obedience in doctrinal preaching. Without a call to obedience, we preach only law that raises the level of guilt or only grace that

produces antinomianism. Even Lutherans are aware of this crucial move. I say "even Lutherans" because the Lutheran law/
gospel approach to preaching has not always presumed obedient
response in action. The reason for such reticence is that Luther
presented only two, not three, uses of the law: the political use
(*usus politicus*), which must exist to hold the wicked in check, to
keep order in the secular state, and the theological use (*usus
theologicus*), where the law accuses sinners, demonstrating their
need for the gospel. Traditionally, Lutheran theologians have resisted Calvin's attempts to make the law more positive. Werner
Elert, in his *Law and Gospel*,[25] attacks Barth for softening the
law, for arguing that the end of judgment is grace. Barth's title,
Gospel and Law,[26] tips his hand. The bottom line for Barth is
grace, and even the law serves this purpose. Elert believes that
this argument is not supported by Scripture, certainly not by
Paul. Elert's argument is cogent when he suggests that too hasty a
move to grace takes the sting out of the law. But it seems to me
that he also overlooks the positive gift of the Decalogue, where
don'ts are also dos, and the way in which the judgment messages
of the prophets are offered not out of God's hate but out of God's
love. Hope always undergirds judgment. The judgment may be
carried out, but a remnant always returns. First and Second
Isaiah belong together.

The third use of the law is the other point of contention for
Lutherans. Calvin believed that there were three uses to the law.
Switching Luther's two uses, he saw the spiritual, or theological,
use first, where the law functions as a mirror, exposing people's
sin, and the civil, or political, use second, as a restraint to the
wicked. Calvin's third use, and for him the principal one, is a
positive use in which the saints are encouraged to live obediently
in response to grace, to "press on" in the Christian life. One can
see this use in his Strassburg liturgy, where the Ten Commandments are read after the Confession of Sin and Absolution, not
before, in which case the law would be used to convict sinners.
The Presbyterian *Worshipbook* follows the same pattern by placing the summary of the law after the Declaration of Pardon. With
these three uses of law—as a mirror, speed limit, and road map,
Calvin talked positively of law. Elert dispels attempts to find a

third use in Luther;[27] and yet Lutherans like Herman Stuempfle and Richard Lischer do so, and argue for all three uses.[28] Lischer does so openly; Stuempfle qualifies his position by naming it "the call to obedience." But in reality, both are talking about Calvin's third use of the law. Both recognize the need for a move beyond the hard word of the law and beyond the good feeling that comes with grace. They see the need for an admonishment to obedience. A look at Luther's sermons will support this approach. Luther himself did plenty of admonishing. Read especially his sermons on the Ten Commandments and his "On the Sum of the Christian Life."[29]

How does all this talk about law and gospel relate to doctrinal preaching in sacrament, season, and creed? It does so indirectly with season and creed, but poignantly with the sacraments. The law and gospel themes are present in both the church year and the confessions of faith. In Advent when we preach Christ as judge and Savior, we are called to determine the place of the law and the meaning of the gospel in our relationship to the coming Christ. Is there a positive side to Christ's judgment? Does the gospel carry with it a demand? The same questions arise with "from thence he shall come to judge the quick and the dead" in the Apostles' Creed.

But the law/gospel motif in preaching relates even more directly to the way we approach, experience, and respond to the sacraments, particularly the Eucharist. First, we are called to preach law, to expose the self-righteousness of those who think they do not need the sacraments of grace, those who live on their own works, like the Judaizers in Galatians or the spiritual perfectionists in the Corinthian epistles. Our churches are full of people like this. Here comes the rich young ruler in a Brooks Brothers' suit, full of pride, but on his knees, showing a semblance of piety. He knows his own righteousness; you can see it in his face. He has kept the law, which means that he tithes. What a wonderful man to have in your church during stewardship time, but Jesus turns him away. The disciples are beside themselves. What they do not understand is that the rich young ruler gives for the wrong reasons—not out of his response to God's love, but to fulfill a law. This man needs the sacrament more than he knows. Like Christ, we preach the law to him, exposing his sin, not as legalism or moralism, which would bolster his pride even more. We preach it to expose sin and show him the need for grace. "Go, sell what you have, and give to the poor." These are harsh words, ones which rich young men of any age are unable to follow.

Yet law sometimes needs to be preached as a hammer of judgment, not always as a mirror of existence. (Stuempfle's insistence on the latter appears to be overstated.[30]) Sometimes both hammer and mirror are in order, as with Nathan and David. The analogy of the little lamb is "mirror of existence," which communicates the point clearly, but without "Thou art the man" as "hammer of judgment," the sermon would have had no impact. Both are needed when we preach law.

If preaching law points to our need for the sacrament, preaching gospel points to its meaning, to the grace we receive in Christ. Preaching gospel addresses those who are aware of their own sin, like the woman caught in adultery. The law had been preached and was about to be carried out with a stoning. But Christ then preached a deeper law, exposing the pride of those holding stones, and in the same moment preached gospel to the woman. "Where are they? Has no one condemned you? Neither do I condemn you."

While preaching the law is addressed to those who think they do not need the sacraments, preaching the gospel looks to those who believe they do not deserve it. Take, for instance, the young Scottish woman who would not partake of the bread and wine because she felt herself unworthy. An old Scottish gentleman sits behind the sobbing young woman. He understands her feelings of unworthiness, for he is also feeling unworthy and is wondering if he should partake of the sacrament. Yet, in a Christ-like way, he leans forward in the pew and, in a whisper that could be heard throughout the church, says, "Take it, lassie, it's meant for sinners." We preach the gospel of Jesus Christ to those who are broken not only by the burden of the law, but by the burden of living. We do so not as libertines,[31] remembering that Christ is indeed both judge and Savior.

I believe that we are to preach the third use, the positive use of
the law, for two reasons. First, we preach law to attack the antinomianism of those who think that once they have been forgiven
they can do what they want, those who think that the sacraments
are all they need. Listen to Paul: "What shall we say then? Are
we to continue in sin that grace may abound? By no means! How
can we who died to sin still live in it? . . . What then? Are we to
sin because we are not under law but under grace?" (Rom. 6:1–2,
15). This call to obedience adds bite to the gospel. Second, we
preach law because the call to obedience adds encouragement;
we preach the third use of the law to lead those who are broken by
sin into a new oneness in Christ and into peace with those around
them. So Jesus looks at the woman, still shattered by her close
call and his unnecessary kindness, and says, "Go, and sin no
more." What a ringing call to obedience which resounds for all
Christendom!

In the Bible and in responsible doctrinal preaching, doctrine
usually leads to decision, concept points to conduct, belief directs
behavior. This points us naturally to the last chapter, where we
look at doctrine and culture, another starting point for preaching
doctrinal sermons.

For Reflection

1. Two adults will be baptized in your parish on Sunday. Construct a sermon using the "six steps" listed in this chapter. For an
example, see Walter Burghardt's "Buried with Him Through
Baptism" in *Sir, We Would Like to See Jesus* (Ramsey, N.J.:
Paulist Press, 1982), 168–72.

2. It is Pentecost season, and you have decided to do a series
of sermons using the theological themes in Pentecost. Choose one
of these themes and use the "six steps" to construct your opening sermon in this series.

3. Plan a series of sermons on the Apostles' Creed. Determine
the number of weeks you will preach and what doctrines you will
preach. Your opening sermon will be entitled "I Believe in God."
How will you construct it? Use the sermon by Luther in the
appendix as a model.

4. Read Paul Tillich's sermon "To Whom Much is Forgiven
. . ."[32] about the woman with the ointment (Luke 7:36–50) to see
the law/gospel, call-to-obedience themes. Notice that they do not
comprise three parts of the sermon but are woven throughout.

Further Reading on This Subject

Abbey, Merrill R. *Living Doctrine in a Vital Pulpit.* Nashville:
Abingdon Press, 1964.

Baillie, Donald M. *Theology of the Sacraments.* New York:
Charles Scribner's Sons, 1957: 141–55.

Baker, Eric. *Preaching Theology.* London: Epworth Press, 1954.

Blackwood, Andrew W. *Doctrinal Preaching for Today.* Grand
Rapids: Baker Book House, 1975: 39–50, 87–108, 150–60.

———. *Planning a Year's Pulpit Work.* Grand Rapids: Baker
Book House, 1975: 108–41.

Braaten, Carl E. *Stewards of the Mysteries.* Minneapolis: Augsburg Publishing House, 1983: 9–12.

Buttrick, David G. "Preaching on the Resurrection," *Religion in
Life*, 45,3 (Autumn 1976): 278–95.

Danker, Frederick W. *Creeds in the Bible.* St. Louis: Concordia
Publishing House, 1966.

Ellingsen, Mark. *Doctrine and Word: Theology in the Pulpit.*
Atlanta: John Knox Press, 1983.

Knight, George A. F. *Law and Grace.* London: SCM Press, 1962.

Lischer, Richard. *A Theology of Preaching.* Nashville: Abingdon
Press, 1981: 30–65.

Miller, Donald G. "Preaching and the Law," *Pittsburgh Perspective*, 8,1 (March 1967): 3–23.

Ott, Heinrich. *Theology and Preaching.* Philadelphia: Westminster Press, 1965.

Rein, Gerhard, ed. *A New Look at the Apostles' Creed.* Minneapolis: Augsburg Publishing House, 1969.

Stookey, Laurence Hull. *Baptism: Christ's Act in the Church.*
Nashville: Abingdon Press, 1982.

Stuempfle, Herman G., Jr. *Preaching Law and Gospel.* Philadelphia: Fortress Press, 1978.

Wingren, Gustav. *The Living Word: A Theological Study of Preaching in the Church*. Philadelphia: Fortress Press, 1960: 137–49.

Doctrinal and Biblical Resources

Buttrick, George Arthur, ed. *The Interpreter's Dictionary of the Bible*. 4 vols. Nashville: Abingdon Press, 1962.

Harvey, Van, ed. *A Handbook of Theological Terms*. New York: Macmillan Co., 1964.

Leith, John H., ed. *Creeds of the Churches*. Atlanta: John Knox Press, 1973.

Rahner, Karl, ed. *Encyclopaedia of Theology: Concise Sacramentum Mundi*. New York: Seabury Press, 1975.

Richardson, Alan. *A Dictionary of Christian Theology*. Philadelphia: Westminster Press, 1969.

_____. *A Theological Word Book of the Bible*. New York: Macmillan Co., 1952.

FIVE

Doctrine and Culture

Anthropocentric Homiletics

The rich theological and ecclesiastical pluralism of the New Testament is evident at every turn. Here is the epistle to the Hebrews, with its high priest Christology; there is the corporate view of the church as the body of Christ in Paul's Corinthian letters. Both stand as models for Anglo-Catholic traditions. The emphasis on administration, teaching, and sound doctrine in the pastoral epistles points to the Calvinist heritage. With the law/gospel dichotomy of Romans and Galatians, we hear the thundering voice of Luther and the church that bears his name. Those sects which say "love your neighbor" and mean their own brothers and sisters to the exclusion of others carry on the tradition of the Johannine communities, particularly the subapostolic churches that stand behind these epistles.[1] They would have nothing to do with Matthew's Jesus, who said, "Love your enemies." This "you and me against the world" faith represents a closed circle.

Then we turn to the missionary activity, the openness to the Gentiles of the Luke-Acts tradition, and we see a completely different ecclesiastical emphasis. In certain ways, it may represent the various Baptist groups, but not all, for some are highly sectarian and withdrawn from the world. Actually, the United Methodist church at points comes closer to the Luke-Acts tradition, but in certain ways it is different as well.

Luke-Acts is worldly, open to the ways of the world, looking out not through stained glass but through plain glass at the teeming market, the worried merchant, the widows, the strangers, and

95

the poor. Luke-Acts churches are actually in every denomination. They make little distinction between evangelism and social responsibility. They go to the world with a living Lord, a helping hand, and an honest interest in the world's questions, with no reticence about arguing for the gospel. This rich mixture of evangelism, social action, and apologetics is everywhere present throughout Luke-Acts. Look at Peter at Pentecost preaching to those outside the faith. Peer in on the Samaritan, an outcast, bending over a Jew! Who could miss Paul on Mars Hill defending the faith, answering the questions of the world? Luke-Acts is the New Testament model for doctrinal preaching in the culture.

Here is our third starting point for doctrinal sermons—not Scripture, not tradition, but culture itself—secular, agnostic humanity. If the purpose of exegetical, catechetical, and polemical preaching is to teach and correct the cynical citizens, the faithful few, the reformers, and the superpatriots in our churches, the purpose of culturally initiated doctrinal preaching is to take seriously the questions of the world and to speak a word of truth to the expatriates, the tourists, and the resident aliens in our churches. At this point I hear in the background the strong, clear voices of James Gustafson and Karl Barth, both complaining about this overemphasis on the needs and desires of modern humanity. They speak from different perspectives; Gustafson calls for a theocentric ethics, while Barth continues his plea for a christocentric theology. Together they offer a collective confession of sin for humanity's major problem, which Niebuhr named for us as pride, interest in ourselves and in our whims and questions. Thus, with their penchant critiques in mind, we move cautiously into what seems to be a blatant anthropocentric homiletics.

Anthropocentric homiletics is a homiletics of the twentieth century, but one that has its roots in the Renaissance and the Enlightenment when the individual became the center of the universe and, as Gustafson has suggested, the tables turned. Man no longer glorified God; "the chief end of God was to glorify man."[2] Anthropocentric homiletics begins with the religious subject, the believer, and, more appropriately in this chapter, the unbeliever as well. With this approach to preaching, not only have we moved away from God and toward humankind, but we have moved away from the Bible and the tradition into the culture. Protestants in their preaching have generally begun with Scripture, and Roman Catholics with doctrine; but both can share the credit and the blame for this approach that begins with the culture.

Although I must admit a certain discomfort with this approach which is prevalent in our time, I do not reject it outright, as did Barth. The Luke-Acts model is too compelling and persuasive. What is important is to understand the varying forms this approach takes in modern preaching and to encourage responsible biblical and theological homework when we undertake a culturally initiated sermon. This will turn a sermon begun with humanity into a sermon that points to God. It will turn anthropocentric homiletics into theocentric preaching.

I have placed this approach last for three reasons: (1) the study of Scripture and dogmatics should precede apologetics, ethics, and evangelism; (2) this type of preaching removes us not one step (as in catechetical and polemical preaching) but two steps from the source and authority for Christian proclamation—Scripture; (3) the homework for culturally initiated doctrinal preaching far exceeds that of the other two types (particularly as one moves into global/moral problems) and thus prevents its frequency. For both theological and practical reasons, we should consider anthropocentric homiletics to be the last approach to doctrinal preaching and the one least often employed in the pulpit.

Questions and Statements
in Church and Culture

Tillich believed that we should listen more carefully to the questions of the world lest we answer questions no one is asking. Culturally initiated doctrinal preaching takes Tillich's belief very seriously. There is simply no one single question (as with Barth's religious subject, Is it true about God?). There are numerous questions that the believer and the unbeliever find troubling— questions about the Bible, about human finitude, about war and peace. In addition, we hear statements that indicate a deep anxiety and hostility lurking behind the face of the world. Tillich saw the world as ontologically schizophrenic. For him, Pablo Picasso and Franz Kafka expressed the present mood, which is one of shock and anxiety. Our world is in pieces, disrupted. Tillich's *Courage to Be* sought to answer this burgeoning fear caused by estrangement. What he called for was not the courage of a soldier in battle but the courage of a human being who, perplexed by the riddles of existence, is still able to say *yes* to life.

This struggle to say *yes* manifests itself in various questions and statements that we hear after worship, in counseling, and especially on a bus, train, or plane. The deep religious yearning of our age emerges constantly when riding public transportation. A clerical collar and an empty seat are sure signs of the potential for theological conversation. Here is Fowler's classic stage four person—that gleeful secularist who has left the church because he or she knows better now. Most of it is myth, anyway. But the secularist still wonders while riding the commuter train day after day, asking himself or herself deep, searching questions—but there is no one to talk to. Secularists are in the pew of the university church. The place is almost empty, even on Sunday morning. But they are there—questioning, hurting, hoping, looking desperately for something. Glib confessions of faith do not come easy for them. But they yearn for something deeper than science's latest offering. They are on the streets and in the shops of small-town America or perhaps sitting alone at home "waiting for" more than "Godot." Some are angry about religion and want to know why Christians believe this or that. Some are even in church. They want help for their personal problems and direction for their moral problems.

Their questions and statements revolve around three basic types of utterances heard in church and culture—three types which we will list briefly first and then address one at a time:

1. Questions and statements heard in church and culture that tend to be *theological* in nature. These are statements like "All religions are alike, so it doesn't matter what you believe" or "Why do the righteous suffer?" These are large and difficult questions which can be starting points for doctrinal sermons.

Some may move in a catechetical or polemical direction, but most in this category are apologetic, answering the questions and challenges of culture.

2. Questions and statements in church and culture that tend to be *pastoral* in nature. These utterances relate to therapeutic-relational problems—existential, personal, and familial problems. Examples would be "How do I handle my grief?", "Why can't I seem to talk to my daughter?" "I can't seem to make it through the day." In some traditions, these questions have sent pastors to their studies, working on next Sunday's sermon.

3. Questions and statements in church and culture that tend to be *ethical* in nature. These could take on the character of personal/moral problems like abortion and contraception, or global/moral problems like hunger and nuclear disarmament. Here are some examples: "If human beings are made in the image of God, why aren't all of God's children treated fairly?" "Welfare is an example of the kingdom of God at work on earth." "Pro-life groups are inconsistent because they support capital punishment."

How is the preacher to tell which of these is worth treating from the pulpit and which not? Three crucial questions need to be asked in order to make this determination.

1. Does the question or statement deserve a whole sermon? Not everything we hear at church or on the street is worth a sermon. The statement may be trivial, not to the person saying it but for Christian proclamation. "The most crucial question before our church today is the color of the choir robes." That is an easy one to identify. Some questions or statements are borderline. "Pastor, my little boy said the cutest thing the other day. He said, 'Everything is beautiful in its own way.' Now isn't that what religion is all about?" This apparently trivial comment carries with it a humanism that is prevalent in our society. On that level, it might possibly open the way for a doctrinal sermon that attacked that position. But if the statement has been repeated by a parishioner, the pastoral dimensions of the problems come into play. Shall we attack our parishioner's son openly from the pulpit? The answer is obvious: of course not. But certainly we would not quote or give support to the statement, lest we commit heresy ourselves.

Another comment overheard could, on the surface, be trivial: "Why do we need to have a confession of sin in our worship service? I am always forced to confess things I haven't done. The preacher makes them all up anyway. Preachers must think we are awfully sinful; either that or they are talking about themselves." Here is a common sight—a parishioner complaining about something. Certainly not every complaint is worthy of a sermon. But this one might be. A doctrinal sermon on the corporate nature of sin and the need for our corporate confession of sin would address this complaint quite well. The communal confession of some of the psalms would be a good place to turn in Scripture. It might seem trivial for a person to ask why hymns are sung in a church, but not to Martin Luther or to the apostle Paul, who "sang hymns at midnight." Woody Allen's "What I want to know is, When I get to heaven will I be able to break a twenty?" is certainly trivial, but in some ways could be an opening for a doctrinal sermon on heaven.

A statement may not deserve a sermon because it is too broad or too large. "Preach on God" is too vague a statement as is "Preach on life." What can you do with those subjects? Not much or perhaps too much. The crucial question at this point is, Can the statement be made more specific or more precise? There are two ways to answer this question. One is by asking the person to talk about what he or she means by this request. The other is to explore the Christian views on this topic and narrow it yourself. The most appropriate response is not to attempt a sermon, but to use the request as an opportunity to get to know the parishioner better.

2. If the question or statement was made in the context of confidentiality in pastoral counseling, should we use it as a starting point for a doctrinal sermon? The immediate and easy answer to this question is no. To preach on it directly or indirectly might breach that confidence and sever all future relationship, not only with that parishioner but with others who might have considered coming in for counseling. Some preachers wisely go to the person and ask for permission. Others argue that even when permission is given, we should not bring these personal statements into the pulpit. Here is a statement that would make a great opening for a sermon on the doctrine of the resurrection of the body: "I want to will my body to science, but my family won't hear of it. I figure it is all over then, but they think my body will somehow be transported to heaven. They don't even want me cremated. What gives?" Again, pastoral sensitivity precludes use of this kind of material unless it is completely anonymous and presented to the congregation that way. Decisions about whether or not to preach on questions or statements of a pastoral nature are much more difficult than deciding on the triviality or vagueness of theological questions.

3. Is a sermon the best forum for the issue? This question has nothing to do with triviality or confidentiality, but with propriety. Not all topics should be addressed from the pulpit. Some topics are simply handled better in adult discussion groups or in public forums open to the community. The answers to three additional questions help us determine the forum question.

a. Is the statement so emotionally explosive that people will not listen clearly and the sermon will offer only heat and little light? Listen to this statement: "Our day-care center has become a real sore spot for a lot of our members. Some want to keep it, others don't like the idea of someone else running it, especially that Jewish girl. I think it is time you preached a sermon on this problem and straightened everything out." Look at the possibilities. We could talk about our oneness in Christ and our roots in the Old Testament faith of the Jews—a direct attack on the anti-Semitism and Marcionism present in that statement. But what good would it do? Some straight talk with this one person would probably be more appropriate. If this position is not widespread throughout the parish, a fiery sermon would only confuse and anger some members. If it is widespread, then perhaps some doctrinal correction is in order. The emotively explosive character of a prevalent problem never held back the prophets. Imagine Nathan before David, thinking to himself, "No, perhaps this is too emotively explosive." Indeed it was, but Nathan was still compelled to say it. Think of Amos's "You cows of Bashan." Hardly emotively tame. But there was a crucial difference between the prophets and the scolders and exhorters of the present era. The prophets preached the wrath of God, not their own. This notion leads to a second question.

b. Will a sermon on this topic find me venting my own hostility or bringing the judgment of God to bear by analyzing the problem in the light of the gospel? This question is less about the topic and more about the preacher. You may think that you are an enlightened person, one who would never get caught in the trap of attacking your congregation about something you hold near and dear. But it is always possible. You may be a former military chaplain, and one of your members happens to say to you, "Pastor, the Bible says, 'Love your enemies and pray for those who persecute you.' But building up nuclear arms is not a way of loving our enemies. Therefore, we should not only support a nuclear freeze, but we should destroy all our weapons, disband the armed forces, and hold daily prayer services for the Communists." Or you may be a pacifist and hear this from another member: "The Israelites believed in a strong national defense, so why shouldn't we? After all, we are God's people. Our coins read 'In God We Trust.'" When responding through a sermon to a statement antithetical to your own ideas, it is important to exercise great caution. If your sermon releases only pent-up anger and not the power and vision of God, then you should reevaluate whether or not to preach it. This does not mean that you have to be completely neutral on the subject. What it means is that your passion and righteous indignation should be divinely inspired and pastorally motivated.

c. Can I do more than analyze, question, or probe with this topic? This question presumes that preaching should do more than analyze, question, or probe. The pulpit is not the place for tentativeness or for mere examination of a problem. "It seems to me" is out of place there. This does not mean that we have all the answers, but only that we can confidently say some things about God and about God's judgment and mercy. Questions and statements that are either too complicated or lead to sermons that make no clear gospel statement probably belong in a discussion forum. "The Bible says, 'An eye for an eye and a tooth for a tooth.' Therefore, the Bible supports capital punishment." On the surface, that statement sounds like one we could correct by pointing to Jesus. But it is actually much more complex. The legal and moral dimensions of capital punishment, not to mention varying religious stances, make it difficult (but not impossible) to handle in a sermon. "Abortion is murder, there is no way around it" is another statement that presents difficulties for Christian preaching.

I offer here no rules, for rules are difficult to defend. We must each decide for ourselves which questions and statements are worthy of the pulpit, which do not breach confidentiality, and which would be better handled elsewhere. Once we have decided in favor of a question or statement, we should ask two more questions: What doctrine speaks to this issue best? and How does the biblical witness inform that doctrine as it addresses that topic? Consider, for example, this question: "If we've got three gods, what makes us any different from the ancient Greeks and Romans with their pantheon of gods?" This question passes the three tests. It is neither trivial nor confidential nor too hot or complex to handle. Certainly it is not an easy question, but it is one that is at least manageable. It is also a question that is theological in nature. What is the doctrine that will best speak to it? Answer: The Trinity. What does Scripture have to say? Answer: It speaks generally of the triune God—not three separate gods but one God. The difficulty with this doctrine is finding a specific biblical text, since it is not a specifically biblical doctrine.

Perhaps the question asked is, "Why did Jesus have to die?" Here is a legitimate theological question. Atonement is the doctrine. Romans and Hebrews, each with its own particular slant, are good places to look for scriptural responses. If the question is, "Why do the righteous suffer?"—certainly a significant question for the pulpit—we look to the providence of God and the question of evil. Turning to the Bible, we might reexamine the life of Job, for certainly Job knew about this question. Niebuhr addressed the problem of suffering specifically by attacking the idea of special providence. He turned to Matt. 5:43–48 where God "makes his sun rise on the evil and on the good, and sends rain on the just and on the unjust."[3]

Once we have established the legitimacy of the question or statement for preaching and examined the doctrine or doctrines that best speak to it and the biblical text or texts that best represent the canonical position, we begin structuring and writing the sermon. We do so remembering that, although all doctrinal sermons are to teach, to touch, and to move, there are different focuses for different sermons. (1) The primary focus of a sermon that addresses a *theological* question is to teach the mind—to answer the question, How am I to understand the Christian faith? (2) The primary focus of the sermon that addresses a *pastoral* question is to touch the heart—to answer the question, How do I deal with my problem? Where do I find the resources within the gospel, the church, and the community to go on? It is the affective question. (3) The primary focus of a sermon that addresses an *ethical* question is to move the will to answer the question, What ought I to do?

Augustinian Apologetic and Read's Rhetorical Approach

Apologetics has always forced theology to account for its own beliefs, "to move out of the mystique of the heart into the full light of reason."[4] Brunner called this "eristics," the act of dispute, not in the cathedral but in the academy and the marketplace. Apologetics is more than Anselm's "faith seeking understanding"; it is faith *offering* understanding. We see it in the New Testament. Paul stands before Festus speaking the truth of the faith (Acts 26:25). In 1 Pet. 3:15, believers are called upon to give reason for their hope. Christians have always been asked to address the unbelieving world, not so much with proofs, but with the truth of what we believe.

Augustine's *City of God* and Pascal's *Pensees* are classics in the field of apologetics. Protestants have not been as apologetic as Roman Catholics, particularly during the Reformation, when they had as the focus of their dogmatics exegetical, catechetical, and polemical goals. But Protestants such as Schleiermacher (particularly in his *Christian Religion: Speeches to its Cultured Despisers*), Kierkegaard, Niebuhr, and Tillich loom large as theologians who have taken seriously the questions of culture. (Barth, of course, would not belong on such a list. In order to identify this approach clearly, we will have to bracket, but not ignore, Barth's critique. For Barth, apologetic theology would lead directly to an anthropocentric homiletics of the worst kind.)

Many homileticians and preachers have moved confidently and directly into uncharted waters, taking on the attacks and questions aimed at the Christian faith. By doing so, they have not only opened new avenues of discussion, but helped believers know better what they themselves believed. Look at the founder of Methodism, John Wesley, preaching Christian doctrine in a sermon entitled "True Christianity Defended."[5] Keep in mind that great Anglican preacher of the nineteenth century, F. W. Robertson, whose apologetic preaching sought to teach positively rather than negatively. Instead of attacking erroneous understandings of Christianity, he proclaimed the doctrines confidently and let the hearers (believers and unbelievers) decide for themselves. The paradoxical ideas of his sermons always made his hearers think. "The Doubt of Thomas" gave modern humanity (with all its empirical questions) its due and then turned to the resurrection accounts to speak directly to that honest doubt.[6]

Who can overlook George Arthur Buttrick standing in the pulpit of Harvard Memorial Church week after week preaching to the nation's most inquisitive minds? Buttrick never bypassed cogent cultural questions; thus, his preaching penetrated deeper and deeper into the heart of the Christian faith. The more he listened to the modern mind, the more he preached the mind of Christ. His *Sermons Preached in a University Church* bear testimony to that fact.[7] In another collection read especially "The Presence of God in an Alien World" to see Buttrick's openness to culture in paradox with his theological certitude.[8]

W. E. Sangster argues for what he calls "philosophic and apologetic" preaching, where the preacher answers directly the large questions of the world: Is God there? and Does he care?[9] Notice the similarity between these questions and Barth's question, Is it true about God? For Barth, unbelievers are asking this question too. The difference lies in approach. Barth will not argue for the truth of the Christian faith. He assumes it and simply presents it to the hearers as if there were no other alternative. There is a certain attractiveness to this method, but it is a method that is not always persuasive to the doubting Thomases of the world. Barth would no doubt reply that Jesus himself did not argue with Thomas. He simply presented himself. This, believes Barth, is what we should do: simply present Christ and leave the rest to the Holy Spirit. Barth's position overlooks the fact that Jesus did debate the Pharisees on numerous occasions—debates that are evident in the controversy pronouncements, the most famous being "Caesar and God" (Mark 12:13–17).

Two alternative positions to Barth are presented by two other theologian/preachers—one ancient and the other modern— Augustine and David H. C. Read. I have chosen these two because they both preach apologetically with theological integrity and rhetorical skill, and thus are good models for those who would attempt to do so today. Augustine's preaching was often either polemical or apologetic; sometimes it was both. In one collection of sermons, there is a section entitled "Pagans and Heretics";[10] it is well named. The first sermon in that section rejoices over "a Donatist who returned to church." The second—on the incarnation—attacks the Manichaeans, Arians, Eunomians, Sabellians, Photinians, Donatists, and Pelagians, thus making it both apologetic and polemic, not to mention rather involved. The most logical and persuasive of the lot is a sermon that deals with Paul at Athens arguing with the Epicureans and the Stoics (Acts 17:16–34); hence, those outside the faith.[11] The major question at issue is, What leads to true happiness? The Epicureans say that it is the "pleasures of the body." The Stoics say that it is the "steadfastness of spirit." Augustine skillfully shows how the two answers represent two sides of the classic human response—that "man looks into himself" for happiness through the body, as do the Epicureans, and through the soul, as do the Stoics. He then shows how these responses, which both point in the same direction, fall short. Neither "pleasures of the body" nor "steadfastness of spirit" fully satisfies. But neither is bad in itself. Augustine will not fall into the Gnostic trap of the Manichaeans. Flesh is not bad in itself. Neither is pure human spirit good by itself. The problem is that pleasure and steadfastness do not go far enough. Only the "gift of God" in Jesus Christ leads to true happiness.

In a single sermon Augustine skillfully dismissed modern hedonism and liberalism by first giving them their due, then demonstrating their weakness, while at the same time preaching the gospel of Jesus Christ. He did so with simple logic, pastoral sensitivity, and faithfulness to the biblical text in the Christian tradition. Not bad for one sermon! The question of culture is, What leads to true happiness? Augustine's theological answer is Jesus Christ, gift of God. But he chose not to state that outright without first taking seriously the answers of philosophy. Admitting that all philosophy and Christian theology are concerned with this question, Augustine then proceeded to the Acts 17 text, where two great philosophical schools were debating Paul over exactly the same question. Not only are these two great philosophical schools, but they represent the whole range of human nature—body and soul. How convenient for Augustine! It makes his argument all the more persuasive.

Augustine reminds us that neither persuasive rhetorical argument nor the use of logic is foreign to Christian preaching. Yet neither should be used maliciously or dishonestly simply to win a debate. Christian proclamation that turns to forensic oratory has moved from pulpit to courtroom. Likewise, since Immanuel Kant, proofs for the existence of God fall short in or out of the pulpit. Deductive logic only works when our hearers accept our premises about God and humanity. But that is not to say that we who preach would not be helped by the study of logic. The informal fallacies of relevance and ambiguity occur frequently on Sunday morning.[12]

Consider the argument from ignorance: it has not been proven that God does not exist, therefore he must. How often has *petitio principii* (begging the question) emerged in a sermon? Here is an example of this circular thinking: "God exists because the Bible tells us so, and we know that what the Bible tells us must be true because it is the revealed Word of God."[13] Hasty generalization (converse accident) is easier to identify: the apostle Paul, a model Christian, was a missionary who traveled the Mediterranean. Therefore, all Christians should be missionaries who travel the Mediterranean. Perhaps one used more often and in earnest is: Jesus walked through the Holy Land. Therefore, all ministers should go and walk through the Holy Land. These are rather obvious examples. Hasty generalization usually appears in much more subtle theological argument.

When fallacies occur, one of three things happens with congregations. (1) They do not understand what we are saying and ignore it. (2) They do understand and do not believe it. (3) They believe it but put the odd thought in a separate religious compartment of their minds so that it does not affect their daily living. Paul Scherer has suggested that people come away from sermons saying one of two things about a particular rendering of the gospel message. They either say, "It isn't true, but I wish it were" or "It is true, but I wish it weren't."[14] The first statement means that the sermon may have been nice, but filled with religious generalities or in-house language and stories; even more, it could have been illogical, not true to life. Perhaps the premises about God made no sense, or the extent of human sin described was trite. Something just did not ring true. The second statement means that the sermon stood the test of human reason and human experience, that it was true to life, and that its grace was so penetrating and its demands so powerful that the hearer left profoundly moved and disturbed—moved by the mercy of God and disturbed by the discipleship which he or she could not avoid.

This turn toward logic does not mean a turn away from the poetic, the richness of language that one hears in a Carlyle Marney, a Fred Speakman, a Frederick Buechner, or a Joseph Donders. Rather, it means a more serious theo-logic and secular logic to give substance and clarity to the heady theo-poetic of such preachers. All the great preachers in the history of Christendom have blended logic and poetics—Augustine, Luther, Calvin, Edwards, Niebuhr, and Tillich. They have had an eye for sound reason and an ear for eloquence. Head and heart have merged. Tough-minded thought has sung with the eloquence of speech presented plainly—"usual words presented in unusual ways," as George Buttrick used to say.

One pastor who understands both rhetorical argument and logical thought in apologetic preaching is David H. C. Read, pastor of Madison Avenue Presbyterian Church in New York City. Read's sermons bear the mark of cultural sensitivity and theological depth. Holy Scripture, the *New York Times,* and the classics of Christian theology seem to inform every message. Read understands the questions of the culture. He has always kept his ear close to society's malaise and discomfort with religion. Read's pulpit ministry has concerned itself with answering culture's questions. It is the primary focus of his work *Overheard,* where questions and attacks on Christianity are analyzed clearly and answered cogently through sermons which were first preached on the National Radio Pulpit.

Read's congregation is not so much his own local parish as the broader public, particularly those resident aliens and tourists who find Christianity an oddity in a nuclear age, and those expatriates and cynical citizens who have turned away from the nonsense of the gospel. They have turned away not as Greeks who sought wisdom and found the gospel to be foolish but because their own nagging and serious theological questions have not been answered. Like Cornelius, they want to know what it is all about. So they ask questions and make accusations. Read hears those queries and those waiting-room remarks. In fact, he "overhears" them, and he speaks to them directly. Questions like "I've got my own religion, who needs the church?"; "I live a pretty decent life. What more do I need?" And statements like "Frankly, I'm bored by the Bible"; "About life after death—we don't know, and I don't care"; "Religion is for the weak, so I don't need a savior"; "I've tried prayer and it doesn't work"; and "I suppose Christ is really kind of a myth."[15]

Questions and statements such as these become starting points

for Read's apologetic sermons. Read's process in preaching them
is first to get behind the statements to understand what they are
really attacking. Second, he identifies the doctrine or doctrines
that speak to the real problem at issue. Scripture informs Read's
approach implicitly, since he does not speak with a specific text in
mind in these sermons. Instead, he speaks as an informed interpreter of the Word. Read's approach is not unlike that of Schleiermacher in his *Speeches*. Read, like Schleiermacher, disarms
"the critics of religion by demonstrating that what they have
rejected is not religion in its truest sense," but misdirected stere-
otypes.[16]

Read's method is a rearrangement of the approach of the anonymous Latin rhetorician who wrote the *Ad Herennium*. This was
a rearrangement that was employed in the Roman senate: (1)
statement or exposition of the case under discussion *(narratio);*
(2) refutation of opposing arguments; (3) outline of the steps in the
argument; and (4) proof of the case.[17] Like Augustine, Read has
been well served by the discipline of classical rhetoric. Following
this pattern, Read's method looks like this:

1. Repeat the question or statement heard in church or culture.
2. List the reasons or proofs for the question/statement.
3. Acknowledge the legitimacy of the statement. (This shows
   that he does not dismiss the statement as ridiculous, which
   would be not only pastorally insensitive but rhetorically
   foolish.)
4. Question the reasons and proofs by (a) exposing a misread-
   ing of culture or human nature, and/or (b) exposing a mis-
   reading of God and/or Christianity.
5. Offer an answer to the question or an alternative statement
   that clarifies the Christian position.

Read's sermon "I Suppose Christianity Is On the Way Out
Now"[18] is a good example of this method. In this sermon the
world's argument is broken into two arguments.

Argument 1
Premise 1:   Slippage in church statistics.
Conclusion: Christianity is on the way out.

Argument 2
Premise 1: Christianity needs to be less exclusivistic.
Premise 2: Other religions that have tried to be exclusivistic have disappeared.
Premise 3: Christianity has served the pre-twentieth-century world well, but it is no longer relevant.
Conclusion: Christianity is on the way out.

Read's reply to this argument is broken into four arguments.

Argument 1
Premise 1: This is not the first time in history that people have said Christianity is finished.
Premise 2: But the church has lasted. The church is an anvil that has worn out many hammers.
Conclusion: Christianity is not on the way out.

Argument 2
Premise 1: Christianity as living faith does not equal Christendom as a society.
Premise 2: Christendom is on the way out.
Conclusion: Christianity is not on the way out. In fact, Christianity may be just beginning.

Argument 3
Premise 1: The answer to the exclusivist claims depends on your Christology.
Premise 2: If Christ is a good man among others, then Christianity is on the way out.
Premise 3: If you have met the living Christ and see him as Lord of past, present, and future, Christianity is not on the way out for you.
Premise 4: I have met the living Christ, and see him as Lord of past, present, and future.
Conclusion: Christianity is not on the way out for me.

Argument 4
Premise 1: Many thousands and millions continue to meet Christ as living Lord.
Conclusion: Christianity is not on the way out. In fact, this is only the beginning.

In this sermon, Read successfully unmasks society's attack, un-ravels it, and preaches the gospel. His sermon "I've Got My Own Religion: Who Needs the Church?" follows a similar pattern.

It is important to note that apologetic preaching does not al-ways respond to attack. Sometimes it goes on the offensive, but not offensively we would hope. Apologetic preaching moves out into the world to inform people and make Christian beliefs clear. Thus Read preached on 7 March 1976, a sermon entitled "What Makes Me a Christian?" Later, in even broader terms, he preached "What Makes Me a Believer?"[19] A Unitarian friend of mine tells me that his church regularly invites Christians and Jews to speak on "Why I Am a . . . ." Read would understand and welcome this invitation. On the other hand, the marquee of Madi-son Avenue Presbyterian Church is an open invitation to Chris-tians and agnostics to explore together Christ and culture.

Read's apologetic preaching is supported by his skillful use of logic, his theological acumen and depth, and his ability, like Schleiermacher, to see through the world's questions to the real, misguided and misunderstood attack on the Christian faith. He helps us clarify our questions and see Christianity on a deeper level. And Read's preaching, like Augustine's, not only teaches but also touches and moves. Down through the centuries the Augustinian apologetic has made for powerful and persuasive proclamation.

Fosdick's Formula

You see it on at least one church marquee in every town—a title that starts with the words "how to": "How to Handle Your Marriage Problems," "How to Have a Better Family Life," "How to Handle Your Grief." The lure of these titles is almost irresistible in an age when books by the same name have become best sellers overnight. The audience is clearly the culture—resi-dent aliens, tourists, expatriates, and even some cynical citizens who are unsure about religion but are willing to give its magical cures a hearing. Who knows? They might even find some help for living in a time like ours.

Certainly that is what Harry Emerson Fosdick was betting on

when he fathered the problem-solution approach to preaching. His devotees have included (in different ways) Norman Vincent Peale, Robert Schuller, and thousands of other lesser-known preachers. Using his method, one identifies a question, either a problem in society or in the lives of individuals, and offers an answer or a solution. For Peale the solution is "positive thinking"; for Schuller, "possibility thinking." This "project method," as Fosdick called it, has also been known variously as "life situation preaching,"[20] "situational preaching,"[21] "therapeutic preaching," and "pastoral situation preaching."[22] Followers of Fosdick like Edgar N. Jackson and Edmund Holt Linn have written books promulgating Fosdick's method.[23] People like Reuel Howe have shared Fosdick's desire to make preaching less monological and more dialogical.[24]

Fosdick made no apologies for his approach. "A sermon . . . should be personal counseling on a group scale."[25] People do not come with an interest in what happened to the Jebusites, but with their own problems, needs, hurts. The preacher, he believed, should speak to these directly. Preaching then becomes a giant group therapy session. Blackwood called it "pulpit counseling."[26] Fosdick did it with great expertise. All over America churchgoers and nonchurchgoers alike sat by their radios, listening week after week to his poignant and penetrating messages. Fosdick had them from the first line. Within a few sentences they could tell that he knew right where they were. His "The Power to See It Through" and "Handling Life's Second Bests" are classic examples of his method at work.

Because of Fosdick's liberalism, his solutions to problems were often humanistic. Christ may be the answer in places, but he often shared the spotlight with great art and great music. Fosdick's Christology emphasized the humanity of Jesus, which pointed to an Abelardian exemplary Christ. But unlike Peale and Schuller, whose "positive and possibility thinking" have become almost purely Pelagian, Fosdick made more room for God's grace in the solving of people's spiritual and personal problems.

If apologetic preaching has occurred primarily in the Catholic tradition, and more recently among some Protestants, the prob-

lem-solution approach begun by Fosdick has appeared most frequently in Protestant pulpits, particularly in some segments of the
United Methodist Church. This approach is well suited to John
Wesley's direct address of the problems of the day in his persist-
ent Arminian theology. But it should also be remembered that
Wesley preached primarily from a biblical text and stayed close to
that text throughout his sermon. In like manner, more and more
United Methodists have recently turned to the lectionary and
explicit expository preaching, although some never left it in the
first place.[27]

This approach to preaching is on the whole a twentieth-century
phenomenon. Christian preaching has always sought to preach to
people's needs. The "golden mouthed" church father, Chrysostom, certainly preached this way.[28] But Christian preaching has
not always started with people's needs. One famous nineteenth-
century preacher, Phillips Brooks, focused his sermons on people's needs and was, in fact, a kind of model for Fosdick.[29] But
Brooks was not typical of his generation or of the generation that
preceded him. Perhaps Brooks stands as a harbinger of things to
come, for the nineteenth century was the century of transition
from religion to psychology, from the demise of Western religious
culture to what Philip Rieff calls "the emergence of psychological
man."[30] "Religious man was born to be saved; psychological man
was born to be pleased."[31] This is indeed the "triumph of the
therapeutic." Rieff asserts that "I believe" has been replaced by
"one feels," and the psychotherapist has become the "secular
spiritual guide" to a whole culture that has grown up under the
influence of Freud.

Christian preaching has always been concerned with the soul of
the believer. But in the last two centuries, the Greek word for
soul, *psyche*, has changed meanings slightly, so that the word
"psychological" is no longer seen under the umbrella of what
used to be a larger term—"theological"—but now stands on its
own. Some people who teach pastoral care have kept the two
together;[32] some have not. It is clear that our culture has sepa-
rated the two. This separation has created a serious homiletical
schizophrenia (notice my use of the psychological term to de-

scribe the problem), which is not solved entirely by Tillich's use of psychotherapeutic language in the place of theological terms. Whatever the case, this psychological approach to preaching is a mark of our age.

There are many problems with this approach. (1) Not all personal problems can or should be solved or "treated" from the pulpit. Long-term counseling is often much more helpful. (2) The problems raised often yield nontheological answers, which turn the preacher into a homiletical Ann Landers, an advice giver. (3) When this approach to preaching only calls upon the hearers to look within themselves for the answers or asks them to soar to great heights like Jonathan Livingston Seagull, then it has not done its job. This is sheer Pelagianism. After reading *Jonathan Livingston Seagull*, George Buttrick had only one comment: "That wretched little bird."

Donald Capps believes that Fosdick's approach has not been specific enough in its relationship to counseling. "What kind of counseling does Fosdick have in mind? Directive or nondirective? Does it emphasize insight or behavioral change?"[33] Capps's critique includes an analysis of the similarities between preaching and pastoral counseling. Pastoral counseling frequently moves through four stages: (1) identification of the problem; (2) reconstruction of the problem; (3) diagnostic interpretation; and (4) pastoral intervention.[34] Using examples from sermons by John Wesley, Martin Luther King, Jr., and John Henry Newman, Capps shows how a problem-solution sermon can and has followed a similar fourfold approach.[35] His analysis is instructive and helpful.

Assuming that we have come across a serious question or statement—a pastoral problem in culture that is universal enough and significant enough to be addressed from the pulpit but not too large—we can now suggest some possible steps for a responsible doctrinal sermon. What will this kind of sermon look like? Following the tenets of sound pastoral counseling, a doctrinal sermon with a pastoral problem as starting point will do three things.

1. The doctrinal sermon will reveal the preacher as a listening pastor. The first and most important skill in pastoral counseling is the ability to listen. A death occurs in the family. The pastor is on the scene almost immediately. Too much talk is not very helpful. This is the time for listening, for a ministry of presence. A person comes for counseling. The pastoral counselor does not immediately launch into the techniques that will help. The person in pain has to talk about the hurt first. The pastoral counselor listens. But even a good Rogerian understands that at this stage there is already some identification of the problem occurring. Listening, then, means more than simply sitting in silence, which would not translate very well to preaching. By focusing on the person's hurt, we show that we are interested, involved, and willing to give complete attention to that person.

This is what Fosdick did so successfully. His sermon openings created the impression that he was listening like a pastor to the hurts of his hearers. He understood. He could name the hurt so well. Fosdick's openings represented nondirective responses to unspoken expressions of personal and spiritual problems.

"Identification" and "reconstruction" of the problem, to use Capps's terminology, includes not only acceptance of the person but recognition that the person has done something wrong, if indeed he or she has. There is no sugarcoating in this kind of nondirective listening from the pulpit. For example, the question might be about the rightness or wrongness of divorce and remarriage. Perhaps the divorced person is feeling guilty about his or her permanent separation and is wondering about Christ's injunctions about divorce and remarriage in the Bible. "How can I remarry without committing adultery, according to Christ's command?" General acceptance of persons in this situation is necessary in preaching. We should begin with an understanding of the problem, and we should also not dismiss it. Our acts have consequences; to ignore that is to misunderstand human sin. Something has gone wrong, and the effects carry into the future, especially when there are children involved. "You can dissolve a marriage, but you can't dissolve a child."

This first stage, then, involves both identification and reconstruction of the problem, the acceptance of the person and the admission that something has, in fact, gone wrong. But if the sermon or the counseling session stopped here, the person in need would have received little help. Identification and reconstruction are not enough. The sermon needs to move on.

2. *The doctrinal sermon will offer helpful assessments that are grounded in Scripture and tradition.* Here the sermon turns from a nondirective to a more directive approach. The goal is to move beyond listening to what Capps calls "diagnostic interpretation" and "pastoral intervention." In both, the Christian preacher examines Scripture and tradition for answers. The purpose is to offer insight that might lead to behavioral change, but not attempt to effect behavioral change by itself.

In some sermons, and when talking with some people, the move to this more directive stage needs to come earlier. A woman with cancer once came to me for pastoral help. Not long into the conversation she blurted out, "I have been to lots of counselors and heard them repeating my phrases and identifying my problem. Don't you do that too! I came to you for some help because you are a man of God. What can you give me?" Rightly or wrongly, I turned to the Bible on my desk and began fumbling for a passage. This woman was ready for more than identification of her problem. She knew her problem. The time we spent with Scripture gave depth to her understanding of herself, her own finitude, her own legitimate reasons for anxiety. This was helpful "diagnostic interpretation." It actually helped her see and accept the fact of her imminent death with more grace and dignity. Her increased understanding of the sustaining providence of God gave her the strength to live in the face of death.

With the divorce question in mind, we need to look more broadly at what marriage means in God's sight. To understand that, we have to look even deeper, to the doctrine of creation. In the doctrine of creation, we see the true intention of marriage.[36] At creation, man and woman were called into a relationship where they are equal but different. In creating man and woman to be together, God has given us a metaphor for his relationship to humankind. It is a metaphor of permanence. Divorce is something that corrupts that permanence. Adultery does so as well. The image is played out in Hosea as Gomer, Hosea's wife, represents Israel. Other texts that deal with this theme are Deut. 24:1–4; Matt. 1:18–20; 19:3–8; Mark 10:2–9. From Deuteronomy to Matthew we see not a legalistic coercion or a blanket acceptance of divorce but more and more progressive attempts to humanize the handling of the problem. In fact, Jesus' intention was to encourage better treatment of women. The sayings are hard, given modern practice, but the focus should be more on divine intent than on legalism.

It should be clear that a sermon on this problem would not be bound by one specific text but by a serious reading of a broad range of passages throughout the canon. It is also clear that more than one doctrine emerges at this point. In addition to creation, repentance and grace should be sounded. Human error may thwart the divine intention in marriage, but it does not dissolve the permanence of the institution of marriage. Thus, awareness of God's forgiveness accompanies confession of sin.

3. The doctrinal sermon will point to resources that will help the person in need. Sermons that only seem to listen and identify, to offer biblical and theological assessment of the problem, often fall short. There is one more step needed—the pointing to resources. The preacher can point to the gifts of God seen in sacrament and church. In churches that frequently celebrate the Eucharist, the former may be more meaningful. With a problem like divorce, the emphasis on the latter, with explicit mention of reconciliation, is certainly in order. Not only is the person's life shattered, but the church often turns its back on the divorced when they are going through the grief process. The daughter asks the divorced mother, "When are they bringing the food, Mommy?" "What do you mean?" she replies. "When Grandpa died, they brought food," says the child. Mention of the church as the body of Christ not only should remind the divorced person of how caring a community the church can be; it should also remind a parish of its responsibility to care and not ignore. A sermon focusing on this could help persons further the process of reconciliation that has already begun in God's reconciliation through Christ.

The preacher can also point in a sermon to the spiritual resources that all people have within themselves, resources that are often untapped. Brooks frequently called on people to remember those times when they withstood trials with God's help.[37] Peale and Schuller do this all the time, quite effectively. Sometimes they give God the credit; sometimes you wonder who gets the credit. But one thing that Fosdick, Brooks, Peale, and Schuller all understand is that "as long as a person looks only at his limitations, his self-knowledge and his understanding of God is seriously distorted. . . ."[38]

Fosdick's problem-solution preaching is probably with us to stay. It is one form of anthropocentric homiletics that is appealing to both church and culture. When done responsibly with biblical and theological grounding, doctrinal sermons that begin with pastoral problems can offer sound Christian proclamation with pastoral sensitivity.

Coffin's Corrective

What ought I to do? Here is the question of Christian conduct that summarizes all the moral questions facing the Christian pulpit. Unlike Fosdick's problem-solution sermon, which has evolved in the shadows of Sigmund Freud and Carl Jung, the homiletical answer to this question of moral behavior has plagued the church for centuries. Questions of justice and injustice are not new to the church. Indeed, they extend back to the prophetic tradition, and beyond that to the law. Believers in the Judeo-Christian tradition have always been concerned with what is right and what is wrong, and how to tell the difference.

Moral problems have often arisen in expository sermons. For example, in the lectionary, the Gospel lesson for The Fifth Sunday in Lent, Year C, is John 8:1–11. Here the question of adultery and what it means in our culture—in contrast with Christ's response—moves one into the consideration of a moral problem. Texts in Luke that call upon us to help the widows, the strangers, and the orphans speak to us of proper Christian conduct.

What is different in the last two centuries is the use of moral problems, questions, and statements as starting points for sermons. We cannot, of course, overlook Francis of Assisi's concern for the poor and needy, Martin Luther's attacks on gluttony and drunkenness,[39] or John Wesley's, Jonathan Edwards's, and George Whitefield's denouncements of moral laxity during the Great Awakening. But the move beyond personal/moral problems into accusations of global/moral sins of injustice coincide somehow with the Industrial Revolution and the abolitionist movement in America. Charles Finney and Henry Ward Beecher are classic examples of preachers who used the pulpit to attack slavery directly in the nineteenth century. The social gospel movement of Walter Rauschenbusch influenced what came to be termed "prophetic preaching" in the twentieth century. Preachers like Reinhold Niebuhr, Martin Luther King, Jr., and William Sloane Coffin, Jr., stand as models of this approach in our time.

William Sloane Coffin is, however, more a protege of his uncle, Henry Sloane Coffin (who in 1915 wrote "Practical Aims of a Liberal Evangelicalism"), and Niebuhr, than Rauschenbusch. Niebuhr's Gifford Lectures (particularly the sections on sin) affected Coffin deeply. Niebuhr's sermons were often more subtle and penetrating than Coffin's, but also less comprehensible to the general public. Nevertheless, there is a similarity of style that even Niebuhr recognized himself. Coffin expresses it this way:

> When I went to visit Reinie on his deathbed in Stockbridge . . . he smiled and growled, "I listened to you on the radio the other day, and I said to Ursula, 'Bill reminds me so of my youth—all that humor, conscience, and demagoguery!"[40]

But the similarity between Coffin and Niebuhr goes beyond style. They both reject political passivity and thoughtless activism and encourage a politically active posture informed by Scripture, tradition, and obedience to Christ. In this respect, both are similar to King.

The "corrective" of William Sloane Coffin is that he has brought together in his preaching the split that occurred late in the nineteenth century between evangelism and social concern.[41] Coffin identifies with people like Richard Mouw, author of *Political Evangelicalism*,[42] and the Christians Richard Quebedeaux

writes about in *The Young Evangelicals.*[43] His understanding of
the connection between evangelism and social concern was made
clear in his address "Evangelism as Social Prophecy," given in
Atlanta in 1973. Coffin believes deeply in the connection between
doctrine and ethics, but he abhors preaching that considers only
the individual and not the corporate community. Individual and
community are inextricably bound together, especially today. We
no longer live in little medieval villages; we live in a global village
that diminishes the significance of national boundaries. And, in
addition, personal problems are frequently entangled in social
problems. One cannot talk about one without the other. The
separation of the two by people like Billy Graham has always
perplexed Coffin. But even Graham has, in recent years, begun
to see the connection between personal and global moral problems.

Coffin's method follows roughly a threefold pattern that is instructive for doctrinal preaching on personal and global moral
problems. The method turns anthropocentric homiletics into theocentric preaching; Coffin starts with the problems of modern
humanity and addresses them with the justice and mercy of God.

*1. Identify the problem in culture; do homework on it to deter-
mine whether it deserves attention in preaching and to understand it fully.* For Coffin, the problem needs to be large, and it
should be controversial. That means that it is probably true to life
and close to the marrow of his hearers' existence as well as a
threat to world order. He would agree with Harold Bosley, who
said, "The only way to avoid controversial issues is to avoid vital
issues."[44] Evangelical John R. W. Stott echoes this sentiment
when he criticizes preachers for being too cowardly on tough
moral problems.[45] We should, Stott believes, address social-polit-
ical issues; Jesus certainly did. The Bible goes beyond questions
of personal salvation to concern for the whole human community.[46] Coffin could not agree more. On Martin Luther King, Jr.'s
birthday, Coffin made it clear: "'Ministers shouldn't meddle in
politics,' was probably first said not to Martin by Governor Wal-
lace, but by Pharaoh to Moses."[47]

Here is a preacher who believes that we should address tough moral questions homiletically. Certainly Coffin wants us to discuss moral questions together, to study them together, and to organize and march together. But the pulpit is not off-limits for him. We should tackle the difficult questions because Christians need guidance. They need to be made to think so that they can be encouraged to act. For this reason, Coffin does not avoid the "emotionally explosive"; he ignites it.

But he never does so foolishly or dogmatically. The reason is that he knows what he is talking about. Not everyone will agree with Coffin's conclusions on issues, but no one questions his knowledge of the problem. Coffin always does his homework. He sets aside time and reads articles and books—whatever he can get his hands on. He reads both sides of an issue. When he emerges from his study, he knows the history of the problem, the political and social dimensions, the various arguments and questions for the modern Christian to ponder. This is all primarily secular homework. Coffin believes that the primary reason preachers avoid controversial issues is not that they have conservative congregations but that they are not doing the homework in order to speak to these issues.[48]

Coffin's own practice is instructive and helpful. He does not attempt a major moral problem every week. In fact, his practice has been to immerse himself in one major problem for a period of time. In the early sixties it was civil rights. In the late sixties to early seventies it was Vietnam. In the late seventies it was hunger and American intervention in places like El Salvador. In the eighties it has been the arms race. Coffin has dealt with various other issues as well, but these are the major ones. He knows that the homework alone on these topics is staggering. At Yale and at Riverside his practice has been to do his homework and make his statement clearly and early to the congregation only once, and not badger them with it week after week. Most of the time he preaches the lectionary and deals with pastoral issues. At Yale he rarely preached on Vietnam after stating his position once and then taking to the streets.

I underscore this point for a reason. We cannot expect to preach on global/moral problems on a weekly basis. We can, however, find one major problem and begin to study it, to learn about it, to become informed critics, and to determine from that study whether to preach it, perhaps eventually doing so. This may take months or, as with Coffin, even years. Members of our congregation then become engaged in the process. Many are already experts on certain aspects of these problems. They would be flattered to help with our study and probably volunteer to lead forum discussions when and if we decide to preach on a certain problem.

2. Coffin's second step is usually to understand the biblical and theological position on the moral problem in question. He has already done the secular homework. Now he turns to the Bible and the theological tradition. Although Coffin often speaks from specific biblical texts ("Vietnam: A Sermon" on Mark 2:1–12[49] and "It's a Sin to Build a Nuclear Weapon," on John 8:2–11 and Ps. 9:15[50]), he would agree with both Bruce C. Birch and Larry L. Rasmussen that there is great diversity in the Bible and that one single text is often too limited.[51] One needs to look at the whole range of biblical statements to get the wider canonical picture. Often the biblical statements seem to contradict one another on various issues. This makes it difficult if not impossible to use one passage as a prescriptive code. How does one preach on capital punishment with the Decalogue's "Thou shalt not kill," knowing that in other places the Old Testament prescribes capital punishment for offenses we would not think twice about today? Here the general sanctity for human life found throughout the Bible must be held in tension with the judicial concerns of ancient Israel and modern America.

With Gustafson and Childs, Coffin also believes that the Bible is the primary but not the only authority for moral discourse. Otherwise he would not do the homework on the secular side of a problem. The Bible is in dialogue with the knowledge we have gained from the natural and social sciences. As Birch and Rasmussen point out, the nonbiblical sources often amass materials

that bring the problems to our attention in the first place.[52] This
has been Coffin's experience throughout his ministry. But even as
the secular sources confront us with problems and enter into
conversation with the canonical witness, they should not super-
sede the Bible's authority in helping us make moral decisions.
Birch and Rasmussen illustrate this point with the example of
"lifeboat ethics."[53] Since everyone cannot get into the lifeboat,
some will have to die. So also in the world today. This is good
pragmatic ethics. But it is also self-serving. Self-serving ethics is
in direct contrast to biblical ethics. Coffin would support this
position. The Bible is not the only authority, but it is the primary
authority.

What makes Coffin so helpful as a model is that he not only
does his biblical homework but he consciously looks for the explicitly doctrinal angle to take. This saves his sermons from turning into humanism, although some would like to categorize them
this way. Like Gustafson, Coffin sees the church as the community of moral discourse; unlike Gustafson, Coffin is explicitly
christocentric in his approach to moral problems. Coffin's Christian doctrine is found at every point. In "Vietnam: A Sermon"
the law/gospel/call-to-obedience pattern is played out thoroughly
as Coffin calls America to respond to the grace of Jesus Christ
and to rise, take up our pallets, and walk. This points to Coffin's
third step.

3. *Bring the religious vision to bear on public life and policy,
and do so pastorally.* Coffin believes that appeals to our common
humanity never go far enough. The reason is that at the root of
our beings we are all sinful. On our own, we are not going to get
together to fight evil. As a matter of fact, some of us will not even
get together at all! Coffin believes that we preachers should speak
theologically about not only ecclesiastical but political matters.
For this reason, he always speaks as a "reverend," whether he is
in a church or the local Rotary Club.

We have a doctrinal message and we should state it clearly.
Here is theocentric preaching in the midst of a theocentric ministry. During the Vietnam War, Coffin believed that it was our

responsibility to bring the religious vision to bear, not to discuss the political ramifications of the war. It was not our responsibility to discuss the constitutionality of the conflict. That is not our turf as preachers.

What could we say? Coffin did his homework. He traveled to Vietnam (something not every minister can do), and discovered for himself how the CIA had been misleading our country. Here is religion's turf. "Thou shalt not bear false witness against thy neighbor." Here is a call to repentance. This is not a political but a theological message. Everyone may not agree with Coffin's theological interpretation, but no one can deny that he speaks theocentrically and christocentrically. Consider his sermon "It's a Sin to Build a Nuclear Weapon," in which Coffin states clearly what Christians have to say about the arms race. "God alone has the authority to end life on this planet—but human beings have the power." Two doctrines—God's creation and sustaining providence, and our threat to both—come through in this sermon. Coffin calls us to repentance and new life—an explicitly religious message. His call to obedience is never framed simply as "Be good," but always it is put in the context of Calvin's third use of the law. Most of his sermons on global/moral problems call us to repentance and new life.

Coffin speaks from a pastor's heart. At times he seems blustery and dogmatic, but he never speaks as one having all of the answers. He speaks as one who cares deeply. His use of humor not only shows his own humanness but, as with Whitefield, it enables him to diffuse tension while preaching the hard message. His sermons call us pastorally.

It can be said that Coffin oversimplifies at times—that nations and other collectivities, as Niebuhr has told us, will not respond as uniformly to a call to repentance as Coffin seems to think. In addition, his creative exegesis of biblical passages gets very close at times to allegory— "Neither do I condemn you; go and build nuclear weapons no more." But Coffin's concern for the church's right to speak on global/moral problems, his straightforward biblical and theological proclamation, and his unquestioned trust in

God's providence echo his uncle's belief that "back of both pro-
test and programme is the living God, and that with him what
should be shall be."[54]

Christ and Culture in Christian Preaching

H. Richard Niebuhr's *Christ and Culture* is indispensable at
this point. This book helps us understand not only whether we as
preachers begin with culture but how we deal with culture in
doctrinal preaching. Culture, for Niebuhr, means society, human
achievement, and the realization and conservation of values for
humanity, which is by nature pluralistic.[55] What we do in apologetic, pastoral, or ethical preaching about culture depends on
which of Niebuhr's five types we represent: Christ against, of,
above, in paradox with culture, or Christ as transformer of culture.

The basic problem Niebuhr addresses is not a new one in Christian history. It is the problem of dual citizenship. How can the
believer live in the kingdom of God and in the present-day culture
at the same time? What is the relationship of the two? This is an
internal problem for every believer. It always has been. What do
we do with "render unto Caesar"? How do we live with Romans
13 and still remain subject to God's authority? We seem to live
with two sets of values and in two countries simultaneously.[56]

In apologetic and pastoral preaching, this dual loyalty appears
most acutely in the way preachers handle the problem of revelation and reason. *Against-culture* preachers see revelation
and reason juxtaposed. Reason is false. We can only look to
revelation for signs of God's justice and mercy. As a result,
against-culture preachers have nothing to do with apologetics.
Their sermons represent a closed vocabulary. They will not
use examples from culture except to illustrate sin. Barth's doctrinal preaching is a classic example of this approach, since he
has no interest in making a "point of contact" in human reason
or experience.

Paradox preachers, many of whom are Lutheran, also find reason to be limited, but do not castigate it as thoroughly. Reason is
all right as far as it goes. But revelation really replaces reason,

since it supplies through Christ what reason cannot supply. Illustrations from culture demonstrate how culture is limited—how the gospel goes beyond culture. Carl Braaten makes this clear in his discussion of the law/gospel approach in Lutheran preaching:

> As auxiliaries of the law, we preachers are free to use everything in sight—philosophy, novels, magazines, newspapers, personal experiences, etc. Our insights into the gospel come primarily from Scripture, but also from the Christian tradition.
>
> The concept of the law in Lutheran homiletics opens up unlimited access to the widest possible range of human experience in the world in the formulation of the questions, whereas the gospel as answer focuses with the greatest possible fidelity and intensity on God's saving revelation in the person of Jesus Christ.[57]

Lutheran preaching is thus willing to deal with the questions of the world, but remains entirely in Scripture and tradition for its answers. Human experience only goes so far in expressing the gospel.

Of-culture preaching represents the liberal tradition which believes that the best of human reason and revelation correspond. Good reason and revelation are in agreement. It is not that David Hume equals the Bible, but close. Christ was the best of what a human being can become. He was a good moral teacher. He was a good person who cared about people. This Christology expresses the extreme—almost Unitarian—end of the of-culture position. Not all of-culture preachers or theologians have this low a Christology. For example, Brooks's and Fosdick's Christologies moved beyond a merely exemplary Christ, but they still should be located in the of-culture position because of the ways in which they often mixed human reason and experience with Christ to answer the world's theological and pastoral questions. Certainly Peale and Schuller belong in this category. Both the social gospel movement and liberation theology mix revelation and reason; revelation is combined in the first case with theories of human progress and in the second case with Marxist ideology. Therefore, preaching that grows out of both of these ways of thinking is of-culture preaching.

Above-culture preaching has traditionally emerged in the Roman Catholic church. Aquinas is Niebuhr's example for this style. Here the best of human reason and culture is not diametrically opposed to revelation. The truth of both comes from the same source—from God. Revelation pulls the best reasoning in the same direction, yet it goes much farther. Reason-as-law might say "Do not steal," whereas revelation-as-gospel goes on toward the same *telos,* the true end of both, with "Go, sell what you have and give to the poor." Revelation-as-gospel may go beyond reason as law, but it never contradicts or replaces law as in Lutheran theology or against-culture preaching.

Paul Tillich is a modern example of above-culture preaching in the revelation and reason category. His use of examples from culture to illustrate not only sin but grace, and his use of psychotherapeutic language from culture to rename the experiences described by traditional theological terms make this designation clear. To him, experiences described by estrangement and healing and new being point to what the church means by sin, salvation, and Christ. The direction in both cases is the same.

Transformation preaching finds revelation and reason in a dialectical relationship to one another. Revelation neither negates reason nor finds it false. Instead, it transforms reason by giving it a new starting point. Transformation preaching shows how the gospel can change culture. Calvin, Edwards, Brunner, and Read are examples of this approach. As in above-culture preaching, illustrations from human reason and experience can be used to demonstrate law and gospel, but here the emphasis is on conversion and transformation of culture. Of-culture preachers, like those adhering to the social gospel and to liberation theology, are interested in transformation, but they have a different and higher view of certain forms of culture. In addition, of-culture preaching's focus is often more on reformation than transformation. Transformation preaching is less related to any particular view of human progress or sociopolitical ideology, although some liberation theologians would argue that even traditional Calvinist preaching cannot separate itself from Western civilization. If in certain cases this criticism is valid, it is more because of the way preachers have related to their culture in the West than because of Calvinist theology itself, whereas liberation theology is by nature more identified with an ideology.

The dual loyalty that H. Richard Niebuhr analyzes is most vivid in church/world or church/state relationships and the problem of doctrinal preaching on global/moral problems. Against-culture preaching would be highly separatist. Since the world (which includes the state) is evil, sectarian preachers will criticize the state and will not encourage their hearers to serve in armed forces or run for public office. Niebuhr uses the Mennonites to illustrate this type of approach. Dual citizenship is not as much of a problem for against-culture preachers. Their hearers live in a new holy community with its own law—the law of love for those within the community.

The paradox, or Lutheran, position handles church/state relationships with the two-kingdoms theory. In some ways, the two-kingdoms theory looks back to Augustine's "City of God" and "City of Earth." As a spiritual person, the believer lives in the kingdom of God. As a secular person, the believer lives in the kingdom of the world. He or she can serve the government, but not criticize it. The believer in public office should have good motives and intentions—and be a good public servant. This is the way the person's religious faith influences his or her politics. Criticism of the government is out of place. Doctrinal sermons on global/moral problems tend to run against the grain of this tradition. Josef Hromadka's criticism of Lutheranism in Germany leading up to World War II was rooted in his belief that Luther's subjectivism—his interest in the inner experience of justification on the part of the believer—and his two-kingdoms theory prevented many German Christians from ever launching a critique against Hitler. Hromadka writes:

> I do not wish to criticize this theory lightly, because I know how difficult it is to detect the authority of the gospel of Christ in public life. I also know how naively some Christians take the affirmation that Christ reigns over the whole world. But when we considered the impotence of the Protestant confessions *vis-a-vis* political

events, and when we saw how easily a deeply religious inner life and a total lack of interest in the situation of the world could go together, we began asking whether this alliance might not have its roots in Luther himself.[58]

This is a serious charge. Perhaps Carl Braaten is right in saying that to draw a straight line between Hitler and Luther is an over-statement.[59] But Braaten does believe that in the two-kingdoms theory the "political and social characteristics of the biblical sym-bol of the kingdom of God have been suppressed in favor of the religious experience of the individual person."[60] Bonhoeffer's own shift away from the two-kingdoms theory into more active political involvement and finally an attempt on Hitler's life tend to support both Hromadka and Braaten.[61] Only a new understanding or a move away from the two-kingdoms theory will open the way for paradox preaching to do more than support governments in power. Perhaps such Lutherans as Richard Neuhaus and John Vannorsdall have understood this problem, for they have ad-dressed the state openly in their doctrinal preaching.

The other three types listed by Niebuhr are easier to under-stand in the church/state relationship. Of-culture preaching be-lieves it is bringing the kingdom of God on earth. The church and world work together in this mission. These Christians believe that Christ fulfills their cultural cause, whatever it may be. The high-est insights of culture and the highest moral insights of Christian-ity correspond. Social gospel and liberation preaching have sought to bring the kingdom of God on earth. Walter Rauschen-busch and Dom Helder Camara are good examples of this ap-proach.[62] Above-culture preaching believes that the church goes beyond the best of the world and fulfills it. Thus even popes like John XXIII and John Paul II have talked about social justice, but not in liberation terms. Transformation preaching sees both church and state under the sovereignty of God. It seeks to con-vert the world to the true good with the third use of the law. Here Barth's criticism of Hitler through the Barmen declaration and Hromadka's wrestling with Marxism in Czechoslovakia demon-strate the differences between Reformed and Lutheran traditions on church/state relations. Transformation preaching does not align itself with any particular political program or ideology, but is willing to criticize or support the government from a theological perspective. Reinhold Niebuhr, Martin Luther King, Jr., and William Sloane Coffin, Jr. are examples of this approach to preaching in America.

The parable of the laborers in the vineyard in Matt. 20:1–16 is an excellent passage to examine in light of these five relationships between Christ and culture. The reason is that a sermon on this parable must of necessity deal with the theological themes of love and justice; it forces us in the direction of a doctrinal sermon that wrestles with the problem of church and culture. The question that comes before us is, How do Niebuhr's five types create different sermons from this same text?

The against-culture and paradox positions are going to distinguish between the ways of the world and the ways of God, the justice of the world and the love of God. The justice of the world in both cases is "each according to his due," "each according to merit," or "each according to his rights." You deserve a certain amount because you earned it—this is the way the world works, but not the way God works.

Against-culture preaching discounts the worldly approach. It denies all forms of cultural social justice, whether through needs, rights, or contract. Against-culture preaching will argue for new relationship only in the context of the new law of love established within the holy community. One might assume that Joseph Donders's sermon fits here, since it seems to criticize the worldly demands for rights. We want "what is ours," says the world. "His kingdom does not work like that," writes Donders. "Right and just fall away against the force that put it into being: God's love, God's sharing love."[63] This is all we have. But Donders is not setting up his own commune. He is not castigating culture in general. He is only showing the deficiency of one form of cultural justice. Against-culture preaching would find nothing good about any justice in the world. In addition, Donders is interpreting this passage spiritually.

Paradox preaching sees the world's justice as "each according to his due." Steimle in "God's Judgments—and Ours" presents a vintage Lutheran sermon.[64] The justice of the world is good. We need it to order our society. But it only goes so far. The horizontal line by which we judge one another falls short. God judges us not according to merit, but according to motive. Intent, not action, is the key here. Inner experience of his grace, not outer show, is the crucial thing. So we live in these two kingdoms, and both are important. Paradox preaching takes the world into consideration more than against-culture preaching, but not as much as the other three types.

Of-culture preaching especially looks seriously at the ways of the world. Liberation preaching does not look at prevalent Western cultural views, but it does focus on Third-World cultural attitudes that lift up the oppressed and the powerless. Liberation preaching supports "Each according to his rights," but it also says, in relation to the vineyard parable, "Each according to his needs, and everyone needs a denarius." That is to say, no matter how much anyone works all receive the same pay. Here is welfare—a system that is designed to equalize and bring the world's wealth into greater balance. By interpreting the laborers hired "in the eleventh hour" as "a group of Chicano migrant workers" to whom the parable communicates "the great justice, not the unfairness of God,"[65] Justo and Catherine Gonzalez put a different doctrinal slant on this passage. Love and justice go together; God's love is seen in justice for the powerless. But notice how the preachers have replaced one cultural perspective (Western imperialism) with another (Third World liberationism).

Karl Rahner's sermon "A Denarius Stands for Us—and for God"[66] demonstrates the above-culture position concerning the laborers in the vineyard, for here love and justice are not different, not contradicted.[67] Love does not replace justice, as in the against-culture and paradox positions. It does not correspond with some existent justice in the world, as in the of-culture position. For this Roman Catholic theologian, love goes beyond justice and helps explain and deepen our understanding of justice. The social justice of "each according to his due" is not denied but extended. Love and justice both come from the same source, but love takes justice further. Interpreting the parable from this perspective, one sees that a contract was fulfilled as it should be: good laws are for the good of the community. But God's love carries good laws further. Social justice is given deeper meaning by God's incalculable mercy: for less than a day's work, more than a day's wage is given. Rahner's Thomistic approach has turned this parable into a doctrinal sermon on love and justice in the classic, above-culture mode.

Like the above-culture sermon, a transformationist sermon keeps love and justice together. There is no distinction between the injustice of the world and the love of God as in the against-culture approach or between the justice of the world and the love of God as found in the paradoxical approach. Nor does the love of God correspond with any particular cultural view of justice as it does from an of-culture viewpoint. Thus, the transformationist will sound most like the Thomist, or the above-culture preacher, in a doctrinal sermon. That is exactly how Read sounds in his sermon about the laborers in the vineyard entitled "Is God Unfair?"[67]

Like Rahner, Read emphasizes that both justice and love are within the purview of God. Both men point out the importance of contracts in our world, of being fair, and of being paid what was agreed upon. Read underscores more than Rahner however, how this contract arrangement is in fact one of the ways we relate to God. The master's answer to the outcry "is a straightforward appeal to legality and justice."[68] Read makes two more points. (1) No matter how unfair the world sometimes seems, God is fair the way the world at its best can be—"each according to his due." This is the justice of God. (2) No matter how much we think we or others deserve, God is more than fair—"each more than he is due." This is the love of God. God's benevolent justice goes beyond good contract justice. In fact, it can and does transform the justice of the world. In this way, God's benevolent justice becomes a model for us to be more just in our relationships with others.

Read takes a different tack from Rahner. Read's implicit modeling of the parable in the sermon is undergirded by his transformationist approach, which says, in effect, "Our views of justice also need more love in them." Read's christological approach, however, paints no exemplary Jesus, as would the of-culture perspective. It continues the transformationist emphasis. Christ is the Savior and Lord who suffered the most unfair death on the cross, one who took "all the unfairness on himself." This unique act of God was fair; it was more than fair. Read therefore says, "the God we meet in Holy Communion is not only fair, he is infinitely kind." The sermon itself has a transforming effect on the hearer and the reader. God's forgiving love alters not only our motives, but our actions toward one another. It not only extends but transforms our view of justice.

In summary, what we have discovered through this section is that the way we preach doctrinal sermons in the context of apologetics and pastoral or moral problems will depend in part upon how we view culture: In what ways do we see the relationship between Christ and culture?

Doctrine Points to Mission

We have come full circle and are now returning to the starting point of this chapter. If the Luke-Acts tradition stands for anything, it stands for mission. Our interest in doctrine and culture in Christian preaching has led us through theological statements, pastoral questions, and moral problems. Now we turn from apologetics and ethics to evangelism. All three are legitimate subjects in Luke-Acts, but evangelism is perhaps the major one. Why do we hold this until the end of a book on doctrinal preaching? Two reasons: (1) Brunner argues convincingly for placing it last; and (2) the primary purpose of doctrinal preaching is to teach the believer; doctrinal preaching evangelizes the unbeliever only secondarily.

For Brunner, eristics involves two exercises: *apologetics*, which is the negative side of theology's concern for the questions of culture, and *missionary theology*, which is the positive side of theology's relationship to the unbeliever.[69] As we have seen, apologetics seeks to clarify by taking the offensive; it shows what is distinctive about the Christian faith. Missionary theology, like apologetics, takes seriously the question of the unbeliever. It is "first of all, wholly concerned with the hearer, his need, his helplessness, his skepticism, and his longing."[70] But its primary goal is the presentation of the gospel of Jesus Christ. Barth would agree with that definition until Brunner adds "from the spiritual situation of the hearer."

Brunner sees missionary theology as a conversation between believer and nonbeliever, where the believer listens carefully to the nonbeliever's position and seeks to address the gospel of Christ to it directly. Two examples, from Acts 2 and Acts 17, are instructive at this point. In the first, Peter responds to the accusation that the followers of Christ are drunk. Peter seizes this as a moment for evangelism. "They are not drunk. It's only 9:00 a.m. They can't be drunk. But let me tell you about Jesus Christ." Peter's sermon makes an immediate point of contact with his hearers, the Jews, by quoting both Joel and David and appealing to the hearers' own experience of Christ in their midst: "you yourselves know this, for it took place here among you" (Acts 2:22, TEV). Peter moves from this point of contact to his message about Christ. Paul's sermon at Athens also appeals to common ground immediately: "I see that in every way you are very religious" (Acts 17:22, TEV). Paul does not attack their gods or despise them for worshiping "an unknown God." On the contrary, he compliments them for their worship and thus skillfully opens the way for the presentation of his God who is Creator and Redeemer of the world.

Good missionary theology—doctrinal preaching that focuses on evangelism—takes seriously the culture which it addresses. It presents the doctrine of Jesus Christ with the questions of the resident aliens, the tourists, and the expatriates in mind. It does so fully aware of the pluralism of the present age. Although Southern Baptists have tended to emphasize this form of doctrinal preaching more, the church universal has always been aware of its responsibility to proclaim the gospel to the world. Evangelism resists denominational allegiance, for all churches point to Christ. From Billy Graham to Bryan Green, this has always been true.

There is another point. The teaching and clarifying in doctrinal preaching is normally done to help believers know who they are and how to act as Christians, but it is also designed to prepare them for their mission of bringing the gospel to the world. This "equipping of the saints" is not only "for the work of the ministry" but also for "building up of the body of Christ" (Eph. 4:12). In this way, doctrine points to mission.

Mission in the Luke-Acts tradition engages believers in evangelism, pastoral care, and social concern. When Jesus sent his disciples out (Luke 9:1–6), they traveled through all the villages preaching the gospel and healing people everywhere (evangelism and pastoral care). When they returned, Jesus empowered his disciples to help him feed the five thousand (social concern). "You yourselves give them something to eat." But this was merely preliminary mission. After more teaching, after a deeper encounter with Christ as crucified and risen Lord, after returning to the Upper Room, they went into all the world. Doctrinal preaching as teaching and encounter with the risen Christ in the context of Christian worship points to mission. Christ, in creed, leads to deed—the final purpose of responsible doctrinal preaching.

For Reflection

1. Using Augustine's and Read's approaches, construct a sermon on one of the following questions and statements:
    a. Why did Jesus have to die?
    b. Christians believe it is all in the cards, so it does not matter what you do. If it does not matter what you do, why go to church?
    c. Christians dwell on sin too much.

2. With the methods presented in this chapter, determine whether or not you would preach on the following pastoral or moral problem, and how you would go about it:

    a. I suppose I will never get over my guilt for not saying I am sorry before she died.

    b. No Christian in his right mind could ever support the death penalty.

3. Consider preaching on Rom. 13:1–7, constructing outlines for three different sermons using three of H. R. Niebuhr's types in *Christ and Culture*.

Further Reading on This Subject

Abbey, Merrill R. *Living Doctrine in a Vital Pulpit*. Nashville: Abingdon Press, 1964: 185–202.

Blackwood, Andrew W. *Doctrinal Preaching for Today*. Grand Rapids: Baker Book House, 1975: 51–85.

Birch, Bruce C. and Larry L. Rasmussen. *Bible and Ethics in the Christian Life*. Minneapolis: Augsburg Publishing House, 1976.

Braaten, Carl E. *Stewards of the Mysteries*. Minneapolis: Augsburg Publishing House, 1983.

Capps, Donald. *Pastoral Counseling and Preaching*. Philadelphia: Westminster Press, 1980.

Coffin, William Sloane, Jr. *The Courage to Love*. New York: Harper & Row, 1982.

Duke, Robert W. *The Sermon as God's Word*. Nashville: Abingdon Press, 1980: 48–63.

Fosdick, Harry Emerson. *Riverside Sermons*. New York: Harper & Brothers, 1958.

Hunt, Ernest Edward. *Sermon Struggles*. New York: Seabury Press, 1982.

Niebuhr, H. Richard. *Christ and Culture*. New York: Harper & Row, 1975.

Read. David H. C. *Overheard*. Nashville: Abingdon Press, 1971.

APPENDIX:

Three Sermons

THE ENIGMA IN THE MIRROR

1 Cor. 13:12

Bruce L. Robertson

Ingmar Bergman's classic film *Through a Glass Darkly* was inspired by this morning's text. Its four characters, David, a novelist, his son Minus, his daughter Karin, and her husband Martin, a physician, are together at the family's island retreat off the coast of Sweden. As the film opens, the camera is offshore, watching as the four tall swimmers walk toward the beach through the shallowing sea. Their images are grotesquely reflected in the waves. Bergman, it is said, considered making the film in color, but after thought he chose to make it in black and white. Instantly, we know that Bergman will outdo himself in plumbing the dark regions of the soul. The film is conceived in black and white—particularly in black.

I'm afraid that's the way it is. Bergman's vision, poetic and probingly honest, is far closer to the truth than the optimistic frippery we often preach.

St. Paul hands us a mirror. What depths are opened as we look into it: terror can be let loose by mirror gazing; vicious self-recrimination can be uncapped; fatigue and finitude are traced in the mirror as are loneliness and the process of disease. Too harsh? I doubt it. At best, what's in the mirror will raise all the ambiguities and perplexities of the human estate. Bergman properly reads the metaphoric sense of the King James translation: It is dark. Unless, that is, our mirror is the mirror called vanity, in which case the darkness is greater still.

139

Another artist speaks to us in a sprightlier, more capricious idiom. David Del Tredici, the contemporary American composer, was commissioned by the Boston Symphony Orchestra to write a musical work to celebrate the Bicentennial. His thematic material is drawn from Lewis Carroll's Alice, who goes through the looking glass. With singing and reading and lots of quirky playing around by the usually staid Bostonians, Tredici leads his audience through the mirror into the realm of fantasy. But the piece oddly enough ends with the orchestra soberly counting out loud in Italian, from one to thirteen. The Italian word for "thirteen," it would seem, is "tredici." It may just be his autograph. But I suspect that the composer is saying to us, "This is fun, but we don't really go behind mirrors. It's all out front. If Tredici stands before the mirror, what he gets back is only the reflection of dear old number thirteen—Tredici."

The modern translations of the Scripture text all agree that Paul was seeing something in a mirror, not looking through a glass. The mirror was bronze and quite definitely opaque.

The newest translation in common use calls what's seen there "a dim image." A better one calls it "a riddle." I prefer *ainigma,* the word used by Paul. There is no intrinsic guarantee that the English transliteration "enigma" conveys Paul's exact intention. But "enigma" says it simply and well. The enigma in the mirror is real to us. For each of us it is the enigma called "me."

The enigma may just have preached an inspired message, but, oh, how very transitory are such messages.

The enigma may just have given both tongue and lips to charismatic utterance, but that tongue and those lips will very shortly fall silent.

The enigma may have been known to entertain high knowledge, hard won, but even that is a fragment, partial, far from the final form of truth.

The enigma may know the law and the word of God, but has a history of denying either or both and all else that's good.

The enigma may love the one asleep in the background, but the most recent betrayal may not be the last.

The mirror of St. Paul's day was precious, a favorite toy of the wealthy, an expensive trifle, a stylish gift. A little collection of mirrors looked well on the table. It is still, in some sense, the plaything of the rich, and we are still enthralled and diverted by the luxury of it.

What do the poor of the world think of our exquisite, lingering fascinations with ourselves?

And you! How does a particularly rocky midlife transition strike you in comparison with starvation at the age of five?

How does a skirmish over seniority in the Presbytery strike you in comparison with death in the streets of Tehran?

Or mod chitchat about sexual dysfunction beside the neighbor's pool with undiagnosed diabetic coma in a shack across town?

The latest tidbits of a suburban divorce with the latest capsize of Haitians or Vietnamese at sea?

God, take the mirror away, lest I wallow in my mannered misery and blind myself to the tragedy in the lives of others.

John Fowles has written a new book, *Daniel Martin,* in which the protagonist, a well-paid actor, begins to doubt the differences between acting and living. Fowles describes Daniel Martin's dilemma this way:

> He divides conversation into two categories: when you speak, and when you listen to yourself speak. Of late, his has been too much the second. Narcissism: when one grows too old to believe in one's uniqueness, one falls in love with one's complexity—as if layers of lies could replace the green illusion; or the sophistries of failure, the stench of success.

There is an alternative to falling in love with our own complexity. I'm tempted to say it is to fall in love with God's complexity, as a deliberate attack on those who make him as simple-minded as they are. We should warn our people against the pious little simplifiers of God, whose lips praise the Lord and whose hands are in the till.

> Tell them he dwells in obscurity.
> Tell them the cloud around him is thick.
> Tell them he came once to a holy mountain.
> And tell them he promised death to any Israelite who dared come near it.

And while you're at it, remind them that Jesus once said there were many things he couldn't tell because we couldn't bear to hear them. Tell them what James Smart said about the Bible: "Just remember, the Bible conceals at least as much about God as it reveals."

Oh yes, God's an enigma too. Going around the desert talking to no one but himself and the prophets, and to them only in riddles. And making people think. Worrying people. Frightening people.

Paul knows this God. He knows the prophets and their problems with God. He was the slave of books long before he was the slave of Christ. He won his place at Gamaliel's side. He had been held to account for every thorny theological thicket in the tradition, and every convolution of rabbinic commentary. The rabbis had a theory (you're not going to believe this, but so help me, it's in Kittel, under *ainigma*—three pages and fourteen absolutely undecipherable footnotes) that the prophets could actually see God through an arrangement involving nine mirrors. But Moses, they said, could see God any time he wanted to with but one mirror.

It would not surprise me if Paul knew the rabbis' theory of seeing God through mirrors, and that in 1 Corinthians 13 he is handing us a mirror of which Moses' mirror was the type. I do so believe, and it is one of Paul's masterstrokes. Here is the mirror by which we see the enigma of the self, and yet it is the mirror in which we see something else entirely. Here is the mirror of the future. Here is the mirror of promise. Here is the mirror of prophetic vision, vision as of the coming day when, like Moses, we shall see God face to face, when we shall know even as we are known. And his is not terror, but abiding love.

Do not ask for more than that. Do not press. Neither rudely invade God's sanctity nor compel him with your arrogance. Rejoice, rather, in his otherness.

Karin, the young woman in Bergman's film, is mentally ill. By night she comes down from her bedroom, wakeful, restless. She goes to her father's study, to his desk, to the core of a writer's privacy—to his diary. She opens it and reads these words: "Her illness is hopeless, but with occasional periods of lucidity. I have long surmised it, but the certainty nevertheless is almost insufferable. To my horror I discover my curiosity. The compulsion to register the progress, concisely to note her gradual dissolution. To utilize her.''

It is the end for Karin. She disintegrates. The helicopter must now be called out to the island from the hospital in Sweden. She will go to the hospital, never to return. And that is a teaching. To live with enigma is bearable, especially when there has been disclosed a future when the enigma is taken away and consummated in love. The enigma is to be preferred to our desire for knowledge we cannot bear.

Sir Edward Elgar once posed a riddle for his musical colleagues. In his greatest work, *Variations on an Original Theme,* op. 36, Elgar dedicates the fourteen lovely variations to his closest friends. Each variation describes the friend; it is, as we say, program music. The hints and the clues about the nature of these friends are quite obvious. Basil Nevinson, the cellist, is honored with a variation that features his instrument. A. J. Jaeger, whose greatest love in life was the slow movement of Beethoven's Sonata *Pathetique,* is honored in his variation with a long quotation from that source. It is quite lovely and it is quite a tribute to the friends of Elgar. The descriptions were all fairly obvious to those who knew Sir Edward's personal associations.

Where, then, is the riddle for Elgar's fellow musicians to solve?

The original theme and all of its variations were written as counterpoint to a melody that is never heard, but is implied in the music. Elgar claimed that the unheard theme, to which the music one hears is contrapuntal, is a beloved theme known to all. Perhaps from Brahms or Beethoven, who knows? The solution to the riddle went with him to the grave, and to this day, as far as I know, no one has cracked the riddle and found the hidden theme in these variations. The London public took the piece to its heart and renamed it *Enigma Variations.*

O, you writers and singers, preachers and poets, don't you know that you are only playing the counterpoint?

JONAH
William J. Carl, III

Jonah is my kind of missionary. Reluctant, withdrawn, stubborn. Never quite ready to go to Nineveh. All over the Bible, people are getting up and going; getting up and answering God's call. Abraham moves out on a promise and a prayer. Moses heads for Egypt with nothing but a shepherd's crook and Aaron to write his sermons. Elijah stands defiant, facing four hundred and fifty Baal prophets. But not Jonah. Jonah stands on the dock with tickets for Tarshish.

All over the New Testament people are getting up and following Jesus. One look from him and they seem mesmerized. Before they even understand what they are getting into, especially in Mark's Gospel, fishermen are dropping their nets, tax collectors are forgetting about credit and debit, and others are leaving their parents behind. A little man called Paul travels the Mediterranean spreading the word. But not Jonah. Jonah stands on the dock with tickets for Tarshish.

Why is Jonah so attractive? Why are we so fascinated with Jonah? I believe there are two reasons. One is that for Jonah there is some one thing that causes him to resist his call. Some one thing that holds him back from a full and complete response to his call. And two, despite God's redemptive liberation, Jonah never really changes. Certainly there is something that holds Jonah back. This endears him to us immediately, for there is some one thing that holds us back as well. We also find it throughout the Bible. Moses may be on the road to Pharaoh's house, but he is shaking all the way. Certainly for Elijah it is fear, for after the scene with the Baal prophets Elijah hides in the cave scared to death of Jezebel.

But Jonah's problem isn't fear. You could understand that with Moses or Elijah. Jonah's problem isn't even with God's call. "I'm ready to preach, Lord, to do your work. You just send me. I'll go. Any place but Nineveh." Now what is the problem with Nineveh? Is it just that it is another foreign land? Certainly going to a foreign land is never easy. When you get there you know you have arrived in a strange place that is unfamiliar.

Neely McCarter, former dean and professor here at Union Theological Seminary, Virginia, is a southerner deepdown. I have always imagined that he woke up whistling Dixie. When Neely went to California to be president of Pacific School of Religion, he knew he was going to a foreign land. Sam Martin said he knew that Neely had left Virginia when once he went to visit Neely in California and got into a car at the airport, turned on the radio, and heard this announcement: "The Gay Liberation Front will hold a rally for the Salvadoran Relief Fund in the Fidel Castro Park at 11:00 on Sunday morning." Sam said to himself, "Yes, Neely has left Virginia; he has gone to a foreign land."

But Jonah's problem isn't with a foreign land, is it? Jonah's problem is with Nineveh. Now what is the problem with Nineveh? Isn't it like any other part of the mission field? Well, not quite. Nineveh was a city on the east bank of the Tigris River, perhaps founded by the Babylonians but fortified as the capital of Assyria. The Assyrians were not too popular in Israel. In the eighth and seventh centuries B.C., they plundered Palestine, looting and burning cities and deporting inhabitants. In 722–721 B.C., the Northern Kingdom of Israel passed out of existence as a result of Assyrian conquest. To the hearers of the Jonah story (and it is a story, but no less real and no less compelling in its impact, because, like the propagandist historical novels of Charles Dickens, Jonah is a story rich with the drama and pathos of human life and human motivation), to the hearers of this story Nineveh was anathema, the object of intense hostility. For perspective, imagine a Southern preacher being asked during the Reconstruction period to go and preach in the church of General Sherman or a Southern Black being asked to go preach to the Ku Klux Klan. "Go to Nineveh," says God. And Jonah says, "Anywhere but Nineveh, Lord; anywhere but Nineveh." So Jonah stands on the dock with tickets for Tarshish.

Jonah really is a narrow little man, a first-class nationalist who believed in Israel first. Jonah is a Zionist who will fight to the death for the Golan Heights, the West Bank, and the Gaza Strip. He is one who sees Israel as the chosen people. And the Gentiles can go to hell for all he cares. How unlike Peter, a Jew's Jew, who, after conversion, is on his way to Cornelius's house. Jonah would never do that.

But let's not be too hard on Jonah, for here we can see the complexity of human nature. We all have our enemies. We understand Jonah. For Oklahomans, it's Easterners; for some Texans, it's Aggies; for Southerners, it's damn Yankees. For Jonah, it's Ninevites. Will Rogers, who never met a man he didn't like, was out of step with the whole human race. Even Jesus had enemies. Certainly he said love your enemies, but I think William Sloane Coffin is right when he says, "Love them as enemies. Let's not be sentimental about this thing."

Jonah is the man of gentle prejudice. He is not killing Ninevites. He is not discriminating against them. He just doesn't want to preach to them. But let us not be too hard on Jonah. He was this way because in the context of our story the Ninevites had destroyed his family. Out of the rubble of the holocaust he crawled, and God called him. God said to him, "Preach, preach to Nineveh."

You see, our contempt for foreigners is not always malicious. Here the fabric of human experience, the ambiguity of human life, displays its complexity. A female seminary student is excited about preaching in a local church. She is called in by the dean of students and informed that the church is very disturbed about her coming because the church has never had a woman in the pulpit. The church does not believe in women being in the pulpit and doesn't intend to begin now. But if they can't get a man, then go ahead and send her. "Go to Nineveh, Jonah, whether you like it or not."

Now what happens next in the story of Jonah represents a paradigm for the Christian believer. It is a pattern for the experience of any believer in the Judeo-Christian tradition down through the centuries. It is a paradigm for Israel in its covenant-making, covenant-breaking relationship with God. It is the paradigm of sin, forgiveness, and the beginnings of new life. Not new life itself, but only the beginnings of new life. Sin, forgiveness, and the beginnings of new life. You see, Jonah is the quintessential human being. Jonah is a classic model of the human species, for there is an ineradicable flaw in his character. One that he cannot erase on his own. It is his desire to control his own destiny and to determine who should and should not be punished. This characteristic is not only the mark of humanity in general, but the mark of Israel in particular. Many commentators believe that Jonah stands for Israel. Jonah in Hebrew means "dove." The dove was a symbol for Israel. Israel hadn't done what it was supposed to do. It had looked into itself too much. God had called Israel to worship and to be a light to the nations, but it had gotten off the track. So God punished the nation. The Babylonians sacked Jerusalem and carried the inhabitants off into exile. Many commentators believe that the sea monster, or fish, stands for Babylon here. Down into the depths of despair went Israel and Jonah. Into exile. Something that has happened to church after church down through the centuries because they forgot their mission.

But like Israel, Jonah was delivered. Delivered from the mouth of the fish. Brought up out of the water like an experience of new birth, new life. And God tries again with Jonah. God still sends him. What a word of grace and challenge all rolled into one! A second chance. Listen to the words: "Then the word of the Lord came to Jonah the second time, 'Arise, go to Nineveh . . .'" The second time! Were there ever kinder words written anywhere? And the word came to Jonah a second time. God never gives up on us. He never lets up and he never gives up. Grace and challenge, forgiveness and responsibility intertwined. Our sin and God's loving call to action are seen in stark contrast here, set side by side, juxtaposed.

Now is the possibility for new life. Sin, forgiveness, the beginning of new life. But with Jonah it is only the beginning of new life. No more. Notice that just as in our ministry and in our Christian lives, this is no Pollyanna story, no fairy tale. Jonah doesn't hop up now and say, "Okay, Lord, it's off to Nineveh I go." There is no dramatic turnaround as with Paul. Jonah is no "new creation" as Paul says in 2 Corinthians. I have sometimes wondered about people who say they are born again. How much have they really changed? Look at Paul himself, "Wretched man that I am, who will deliver me from this body of death?" This is real human drama. Jonah remains in character, as if some Augustinian or Niebuhrian playwright has got hold of the story. He goes to Nineveh, but drags his feet all the way. He goes reluctantly. There is a hint of thankfulness, but the order still looms large.

The superior officer asks his sergeant to do something and the sergeant, like Jonah, says, "Is that an order, sir?" "Yes, it is," is the reply. "Well, if you put it that way, yes, sir." The child is asked by the parent to go welcome the new girl on the block and be nice to her. The child says, "Do I have to, Mommy?" "Yes." We are told to welcome to worship those we would just as soon not have in our church. Must we go? Yes. We are invited to sit at table in the presence of the risen Christ with people we would not normally invite to our own homes for dinner. "Thou preparest a table before me in the presence of mine enemies."

I remember sitting in the St. Louis airport for hours when I was in seminary. And I remember once sitting next to a young man who looked particularly tired and distraught. Having finished a semester of CPE [Clinical Pastoral Education], I looked at him and said, "Young man, you look particularly tired and distraught." And, as a matter of fact, he told me he was. I thought, "Boy, have I got somebody to work on here." He told me he was a Mormon, just home from his two-year stint. He said he was pooped. He was tired of riding those bikes and wearing those skinny little black ties. But he had no choice. Everyone in his church had to do missionary work. Everyone had to go to Nineveh.

So off goes Jonah, half-heartedly, half-hoping that no one in Nineveh will respond and God will level the city with his mighty wrath. Jonah, the reluctant preacher, stumbled into town half hoping to get ignored or kicked out; and lo and behold, the whole town came forth, singing "Just as I am, without one plea." He didn't know what to do with them all. Jonah wanted God to blow the whole place sky high. "Punish them," he said. "I know I am the righteous one; they are the sinners." In the 1970s, when a tornado came through a certain city, it really hit one of the seminaries there. One person commented on the fact that the preachers from that seminary had been preaching vehemently against the red light district downtown, and that when the tornado came through, it missed the red light district but hit the seminary. "I am the righteous one," said Jonah. "They are the sinners."

Jonah never could understand about God's great forgiveness. Like some preachers, he only saw God as a giant frown in the sky. He never quite understood that there is a wideness to God's mercy.

There are some who understand this, though. Those whose love for their enemies transcends human hatred. It is a love that is hard to comprehend. I suppose I will never completely understand Jonathan Masango, the black South African pastor who once studied in the United States. I suppose I will never understand his forgiveness, his openness, as he headed back to South Africa, as he headed back to Nineveh and the probability of prison. Unlike Jonah, Masango has a vision of the wideness of God's mercy that carries him beyond the hatred he feels for the Africaaner. For his model is not Jonah, but Jesus, and his motto is not "Punish them" but "Forgive them, Lord, for they know not what they do."

To the end, Jonah, like King Lear, remained a tragic character. He remained in character to the end. But you don't have to. The good news is this: in Christ you can become a new person altogether. For you see, you are made in God's image and, by his grace, made to open your heart to others.

THE CREED*
Martin Luther

You have heard the first part of Christian doctrine, namely, the Ten Commandments. And I have carefully admonished you to

*Reprinted from *Sermons*, vol. 51 of *Luther's Works* (St. Louis: Concordia Publishing House; Philadelphia: Fortress Press, 1959), 162–69.

exhort your household to learn them word for word, that they should then obey God and you as their masters, and that you too should obey God. For if you teach and urge your families, things will go forward. There has never yet been a [perfect] learned man; the more he has studied the more learned he has become. (Here he recited the Ten Commandments in order.)

Now we shall take up the second part. In former times you heard preaching on twelve articles of the Creed. If anybody wants to divide it up, he could find even more. You, however, should divide the Creed into the main parts indicated by the fact that there are three persons: God the Father, Son, and Holy Spirit; since I believe in God the Father, I believe in God the Son, and I believe in God the Holy Spirit, who are one God. Thus you can divide each separate article into its parts. The first article teaches creation, the second redemption, the third sanctification. The first, how we are created together with all creatures; the second, how we are redeemed; the third, how we are to become holy and pure and live and continue to be pure. The children and uneducated people should learn this in the simplest fashion: the Creed has three articles, the first concerning the Father, the second concerning the Son, the third concerning the Holy Spirit. What do you believe about the Father? Answer: He is the creator. About the Son? He is the redeemer. About the Holy Spirit? He is the sanctifier. For educated people one could divide the articles into as many parts as there are words in it. But now I want to teach the uneducated and the children.

[The First Article]

The first article teaches that God is the Father, the creator of heaven and earth. What is this? What do these words mean? The meaning is that I should believe that I am God's creature, that he has given to me body, soul, good eyes, reason, a good wife, children, fields, meadows, pigs, and cows, and besides this, he has given to me the four elements, water, fire, air, and earth. Thus this article teaches that you do not have your life of yourself, not even a hair. I would not even have a pig's ear, if God had not created it for me. Everything that exists is comprehended in that little word "creator." Here we could go on preaching at length about how the world, which also says, I believe in God, believes this. Therefore, everything you have, however small it may be, remember this when you say "creator," even if you set great store by it. Do not let us think that we have created ourselves, as the proud princes do.

At this time I speak only of these things, for the creator, the Father almighty, has still more in store [than I can enumerate here]. I believe that he has given to me my life, my five senses, reason, wife, and children. None of these do I have of myself. God is the "creator," that is, God has given everything, body and soul, including every member of the body. But if everything is the gift of God, then you owe it to him to serve him with all these things and praise and thank him, since he has given them and still preserves them. But, I ask you, how many are there in the world who understand this word "creator"? For nobody serves him. We sin against God with all our members, one after another, with wife, children, house, home.

Therefore, this first article might well humble and terrify us, since we do not believe it. Note that I am basing [everything] on the word "creator," that is, I believe that God has given to me body and soul, the five senses, clothing, food, shelter, wife, child, cattle, land. It follows from this that I should serve, obey, praise and thank him. A man who believes this article and looks at his cow says: This the Lord gave to me; and he says the same with regard to wife and children.

In short, the first article teaches creation, the second redemption, the third sanctification. The creation, it teaches, means that I believe that God has given to me body, life, reason, and all that I possess. These things I have not of myself, that I may not become proud. I cannot either give them to myself or keep them by myself. But why has he given them to you and what do you think he gave them to you for? In order to found monasteries? No, in order that you should praise him and thank him. There are many who say these words, "I believe in God the Father," but do not understand what these words mean.

"And in Jesus Christ"

You have heard that for the simple and the children we divide the Creed into three articles. The first part deals with the Father, the second with the Son, the third with the Holy Spirit. The first teaches creation, the second redemption, the third sanctification, in order that each may know what he is saying when he says the Creed. I have emphasized the word "creator" in order that, when you are asked, you may answer: I believe that God is the creator, who has given to me my body and soul, all members, all physical goods, all possessions. Therefore I owe it to him to serve, thank, and praise him. This first article requires that you believe. This is most certainly true.

Now follows the second article. This too we want to treat for the children and I shall emphasize only the words "our Lord." If you are asked, What do you mean when you say, "I believe in Jesus Christ"? answer: I mean by this that I believe that Jesus Christ, the true Son of God, has become my Lord. How? By freeing me from death, sin, hell, and all evil. For before I had no king and lord; the devil was our lord and king; blindness, death, sin, the flesh, and the world were our lords whom we served. Now they have all been driven out and in their stead there has been given to us the Lord Christ, who is the Lord of righteousness, salvation, and all good. And this article you hear preached constantly, especially on Sundays, as for example, "Behold, your king is coming to you." Therefore, you must believe in Jesus, that he has become your Lord, that is, that he has redeemed you from death and sin and received you into his bosom. Therefore I have rightly said that the first article teaches the creation and the second redemption. For after we had been created, the devil deceived us and became our Lord. But now Christ frees us from death, the devil, and sin and gives us righteousness, life, faith, power, salvation, and wisdom.

It is because of this article that we are called Christians, for those who acknowledge and call upon Christ are called Christians. But the words which follow, "conceived by the Holy Ghost, born of the Virgin Mary," etc., are points which emphasize and show what Christ became, what he did as our Lord in order to redeem us, what it cost him, what he risked. This is what happened: He was conceived by the Holy Spirit without any sin whatsoever in order that he might become my Lord and redeem me. He did it all in order to become my Lord, for he must be so holy that the devil could have no claim upon him. These points show what kind of a God he is and what he paid in order that I might come under his lordship, namely, his own body, with which he established his kingdom. The whole gospel is contained in this article, for the gospel is nothing else but the preaching of Christ, who was conceived, born, [raised again, ascended, and so on].

Therefore learn to understand these words "our Lord." I should believe and I do believe that Christ is my Lord, that is, the one who has redeemed me, for the second article says that he has conquered death and sin and liberated me from them. At first, when I was created, I had all kinds of goods, body, [soul, etc.]; but I served sin, death, and the devil. Then came Christ, who suffered death in order that I might be free from death and become his child and be led to righteousness and to life. Thus the word "Lord" here is equivalent to the word "Redeemer."

The other points show what it was by which he accomplished this and what a price he paid for it, namely, not with gold, silver, or an army of knights, but with his own self, that is, with his own body. He was conceived by the Holy Spirit, born of the Virgin Mary, and so on. I shall not say any more about this article because I do not want to overwhelm you. It is true Christian article, which neither the Jews nor the papists nor the sectarians believe. For he who believes that he will be saved by his own works and not through Christ [does not believe that Christ is his Lord]. This belongs to the regular preaching.

In these two parts we have heard what we have received from the Father and from the Son, namely, from the Father creation, from the Son redemption.

"I believe in the Holy Ghost"

The third article is about the Holy Spirit, who is one God with the Father and the Son. His office is to make holy or to vivify. Here again one must understand the words, "Holy Spirit," what "Holy Spirit" means, for there is the human spirit, evil spirits, and the Holy Spirit. Here he is called the "Holy Spirit." Why is he so called? Because he sanctifies. And therefore I believe in the Holy Spirit, because he has sanctified me and still sanctifies me. How does this happen? In this way; just as the Son accepts and receives his lordship through his death, so the Holy Spirit sanctifies through the following parts. In the first place he has led you into the holy, catholic church and placed you in the bosom of the church. But in that church he preserves [you] and through it he preaches and brings you [to Christ] through the Word. Christ gained his lordship through death; but how do I come to it? If [his] work remains hidden, then it is lost. So, in order that Christ's death and resurrection may not remain hidden, the Holy Spirit comes and preaches, that is, the Holy Spirit leads you to the Lord, who redeems you. So if I ask you: What does this article mean? answer: I believe that the Holy Spirit sanctifies me. So, as the Father is my creator and Christ is my Lord, so the Holy Spirit is my sanctifier. For he sanctifies me through the following works: through "the forgiveness of sins, the resurrection of the body, and the life everlasting."

The Christian church is your mother, who gives birth to you and bears you through the Word. And this is done by the Holy Spirit who bears witness concerning Christ. Under the papacy nobody preached that Christ is my Lord in the sense that I would be saved without my works. There it was an evil and human spirit that was preaching. That spirit preaches Christ, it is true, but along with it, preaches works, that through them a man is saved. The Holy Spirit, however, sanctifies by leading you into the holy church and proclaiming to you the Word which the Christian church proclaims.

"The communion of saints." This is of one piece with the preceding. Formerly it was not in the Creed. When you hear the word "church" understand that it means group *[Haufe]*, as we say in German, the Wittenberg group or congregation *[Gemeine]*, that is, a holy, Christian group, assembly, or, in German, the holy, common church, and it is a word which should not be called "communion" *[Gemeinschaft]*, but rather "a congregation" *[eine Gemeine]*. Someone wanted to explain the first term, "catholic church" [and added the words] *communio sanctorum*, which in German means a congregation of saints, that is, a congregation made up only of saints. "Christian church" and "congregation of saints" are one and the same thing. In other words: I believe that there is a holy group and a congregation made up only of saints. And you too are in this church; the Holy Spirit leads you into it through the preaching of the gospel. Formerly you knew nothing of Christ, but the Christian church proclaimed Christ to you. That is, I believe that there is a holy church *[sanctam Christianitatem]*, which is a congregation in which there are nothing but saints. Through the Christian church, that is, through its ministry *[officium]*, you were sanctified; for the Holy Spirit uses its ministry in order to sanctify you. Otherwise you would never know and hear Christ.

Then, in this Christian church, you have "the forgiveness of sins." This term includes baptism, consolation upon a deathbed, the sacrament of the altar, absolution, and all the comforting passages [of the gospel]. In this term are included all the ministrations through which the church forgives sins, especially where the gospel, not laws or traditions, is preached. Outside of this church and these sacraments and [ministrations] there is no sanctification. The clerics are outside the church, because they want to be saved through their works. Here we would need to preach about these individually.

The third point is that the Holy Spirit will sanctify you through "the resurrection of the flesh." As long as we live here [on earth] we continue to pray, "Forgive us our trespasses, as we forgive those who trespass against us"; but after death sin will have completely passed away and then the Holy Spirit will complete his work and then my sanctification will be complete. Therefore it will also be life and nothing but life.

This is a brief explanation of the third article, but for you it is obscure, because you do not listen to it. The third article, therefore, is that I believe in the Holy Spirit, that is, that the Holy Spirit will sanctify me and is sanctifying me. Therefore, from the Father I receive creation, from the Son redemption, from the Holy Spirit sanctification. How does he sanctify me? By causing me to believe that there is one, holy church through which he sanctifies me, through which the Holy Spirit speaks and causes the preachers to preach the gospel. The same he gives to you in your heart through the sacraments, that you may believe the Word and become a member of the church. He begins to sanctify now; when we have died, he will complete this sanctification through both "the resurrection of the body" and "the life everlasting." When we [Germans] hear the word "flesh," we immediately think that what is being spoken of is flesh in a meat market. What the Hebrews called "flesh," we call "body"; hence, I believe that our body will rise from death and thus live eternally. Then we will be interred and buried "in dishonor," as 1 Cor. 15 [:43] says, but will be raised "in glory."

These latter clauses show the ways in which he sanctifies me, for the Holy Spirit does not justify you outside of the church, as the fanatics, who creep into corners, think. Therefore immediately after the Holy Spirit is placed the Christian church, in which all his gifts are to be found. Through it he preaches, calls you and makes Christ known to you, and breathes into you the faith that, through the sacraments and God's Word, you will be made free from sin and thus be totally free on earth. When you die, remaining in the church, then he will raise you up and sanctify you wholly. The apostles called him the Holy Spirit because he makes everything holy and does everything in Christendom and through the church. On the other hand, an evil spirit does the opposite. The creation we have had long since and Christ has fulfilled his office; but the Holy Spirit is still at work, because the forgiveness of sins is still not fully accomplished. We are not yet freed from death, but will be after the resurrection of the flesh.

I believe in God, that he is my creator, in Jesus Christ, that he is my Lord, in the Holy Spirit, that he is my sanctifier. God has created me and given me life, soul, body, and all goods; Christ has brought me into his lordship through his body; and the Holy Spirit sanctifies me through his Word and the sacraments, which are in the church, and will sanctify us wholly on the last day. This teaching is different from that of the commandments. The commandments teach what we should do, but the Creed teaches what we have received from God. The Creed, therefore, gives that which you need. This is the Christian faith: to know what you must do and what has been given to you.

NOTES

ONE

1. Eric Baker, *Preaching Theology* (London: Epworth Press, 1954), 7.
2. W. E. Sangster, *Doctrinal Preaching: Its Neglect and Recovery* (Birmingham, England: Berean Press, 1953), 4.
3. Friedrich Schleiermacher, *Brief Outline on the Study of Theology*, trans. Terrence N. Tice (Atlanta: John Knox Press, 1977), 116.
4. Ibid., 79–80.

TWO

1. Reginald Fuller, *The Foundations of New Testament Christology* (New York: Charles Scribner's Sons, 1965).
2. Karl Barth, *The Word of God and the Word of Man*, trans. Douglas Horton (Gloucester, Mass.: Peter Smith, 1978), 107–12.
3. Leander Keck imparted this information in a lecture given at Union Theological Seminary, Richmond, Va., July 1977.
4. Gerhard Ebeling, *God and Word* (Philadelphia: Fortress Press, 1967), 34–35.
5. Jacques Ellul, *The New Demons*, trans. C. Edward Hopkin (New York: Seabury Press, 1975), 205.
6. Ibid., 40.
7. Fred Craddock, *Overhearing the Gospel* (Nashville: Abingdon Press, 1978).
8. Ibid., 33–34.
9. James W. Fowler, *Stages of Faith* (New York: Harper & Row, 1981), 151–73.
10. Ibid., 174–83.
11. Although this group would approximate Fowler's stage five, I would describe it in a different way. I find stages five and six in Fowler's book the most difficult to document and understand. His ambivalence at the beginning of his discussion of conjunctive faith indicates a similar difficulty. There are other places also at which Fowler can be criticized; for instance, see Craig Dykstra, *Vision and Character: A Christian Educator's Alternative to Kohlberg* (Ramsey, N.J.: Paulist Press, 1981). But

all in all, I believe that Fowler has offered a helpful description of the phenomenon of religious experience.

12. Ian Pitt-Watson, *Preaching: A Kind of Folly* (Philadelphia: Westminster Press, 1976).

13. Karl Barth, *The Preaching of the Gospel*, trans. B. E. Hooke (Philadelphia: Westminster Press, 1963), 54.

14. Ibid., 21.

15. Karl Barth, *Prayer and Preaching* (London: SCM Press, 1964), 100.

16. Barth, *The Preaching of the Gospel*, 52.

17. Paul Tillich, *Theology of Culture* (New York and London: Oxford University Press, 1972), 212.

18. Pitt-Watson, *Preaching*, 37–40.

19. John Smith, *The Analogy of Experience* (New York: Harper & Row, 1973), xi–xx.

20. Ibid.

21. Craddock, *Overhearing the Gospel*.

22. Tillich, *Theology of Culture*, 202, 207.

23. Edmund Steimle, "The Preached Word in Action" (Taped lecture, 1960).

24. Ibid.

25. Merrill R. Abbey, *Living Doctrine in a Vital Pulpit* (Nashville: Abingdon Press, 1964), 59.

26. David G. Buttrick, "Homiletics and Rhetoric" (Lecture delivered at Pittsburgh Theological Seminary, 16 April 1979).

27. Eugen Rosenstock-Huessy, *The Christian Future* (New York: Harper & Row, 1966), 166.

28. Hans Küng, *On Being a Christian,* trans. Edward Quinn (New York: Doubleday & Co., 1976), 576–81.

29. Jürgen Moltmann, *The Crucified God* (New York: Harper & Row, 1973).

30. Robert Howard Clausen examines Arthur Miller's *After the Fall* and *The Price,* John James Osborne's *Inadmissible Evidence,* Edward Albee's *A Delicate Balance*, Frank D. Gilroy's *The Subject Was Roses,* and Eugene Ionesco's *Exit the King* in *The Cross and the Cries of Human Need* (Minneapolis: Augsburg Publishing House, 1973).

31. Friedrich Schleiermacher, *The Christian Faith* (Philadelphia: Fortress Press, 1976; Edinburgh: T. & T. Clark, 1968), 78–79.

32. Ian Ramsey, *Religious Language* (New York: Macmillan Co.; London: SCM Press, 1957), 180.

THREE

1. James S. Stewart, "Expository Preaching," *Preaching from Doctrine* (Lecture delivered at Union Theological Seminary, Richmond, Va., August 1955).

2. Andrew W. Blackwood, *Doctrinal Preaching for Today* (Grand Rapids: Baker Book House, 1975), 125, and Donald G. Miller, *The Way to Biblical Preaching* (Nashville: Abingdon Press, 1957), 72–75.

3. Emil Brunner, *The Christian Doctrine of God,* trans. Olive Wyon (Philadelphia: Westminster Press, 1950), 1:93–96.

4. Brevard Childs, *Biblical Theology in Crisis* (Philadelphia: Westminster Press, 1970).

5. William Evans, *The Great Doctrines of the Bible* (Chicago: The Bible Institute Colportage Association, 1912) and Benjamin Breckinridge Warfield, *Biblical Doctrines* (New York: Oxford University Press, 1929).

6. Rudolf Bultmann, *Theology of the New Testament,* trans. Kendrick Grobel (New York: Charles Scribner's Sons, 1970); Millar Burrows, *An Outline of Biblical Theology* (Philadelphia: Westminster Press, 1956); Walter Eichrodt, *Theology of the Old Testament,* 2 vols. (Philadelphia: Westminster Press; London: SCM Press, 1961, 1967); Edmond Jacob, *Theology of the Old Testament* (New York: Harper & Row, 1958); Gerhard von Rad, *Old Testament Theology,* 2 vols. (New York: Harper & Row; Edinburgh: Oliver & Boyd, 1962, 1965).

7. James Barr, *Old and New in Interpretation: A Study of the Two Testaments* (London: SCM Press, 1966).

8. Childs, *Biblical Theology,* 101, 114.

9. Ibid., 143, 146.

10. Wilfrid J. Harrington, *The Path of Biblical Theology* (Dublin: Gill and Macmillan, 1973), 380–82.

11. Donald E. Gowan, *Reclaiming the Old Testament for the Christian Pulpit* (Atlanta: John Knox Press, 1980).

12. Gerhard von Rad, *Genesis: A Commentary,* trans. John H. Marks (Philadelphia: Westminster Press, 1961), 34–35.

13. Theodore O. Wedel, *The Pulpit Rediscovers Theology* (New York: Seabury Press, 1956), 95–100.

14. Joseph A. Fitzmyer, *Pauline Theology* (Englewood Cliffs, N.J.: Prentice-Hall, 1966), 1–4.

15. Fred B. Craddock, *The Gospels* (Nashville: Abingdon Press, 1981), 17.

16. Robert Crotty and Gregory Manly, *Commentaries on the Readings of the Lectionary* (New York: Pueblo Publishing Company, 1975); Reginald H. Fuller, *Preaching the New Lectionary: The Word of God for the Church Today* (Collegeville, Minn.: The Liturgical Press, 1974).

17. Gerard F. Sloyan, *A Commentary on the New Lectionary* (Ramsey, N.J.: Paulist Press, 1975).

18. Both Proclamation 1 and Proclamation 2 consist of twenty-four volumes in three series designated A, B, and C which correspond to the cycles of the three-year lectionary. Proclamation 1 has two volumes covering the lesser festivals; Proclamation 2 has four. Proclamation 3,

which has only one author per volume, is currently being produced. All
are published by Fortress Press.

19. Gerard F. Sloyan, "The Lectionary as a Context for Interpretation," *Interpretation* 31,2 (April 1977): 137.

20. Ibid., 137–38.

21. Joseph Ford Newton, *Come, Holy Spirit: Sermons by Karl Barth
and Eduard Thurneysen,* trans. George W. Richards (New York: Round
Table Press, 1934), xiv.

22. H. Grady Davis, *Design for Preaching* (Philadelphia: Fortress
Press, 1973), 63.

23. John Calvin, *The Deity of Christ and Other Sermons,* trans. Leroy
Nixon (Grand Rapids: Wm. B. Eerdmans, 1950), 32.

24. Publisher's introduction, *John Calvin's Sermons on the Epistle to
the Ephesians* (Carlisle, Pa.: Banner of Truth Trusts, 1975), 2.

25. *The Works of President Edwards* (New York: Robert Carter and
Brothers, 1879), 4:179–201.

26. Clyde E. Fant, Jr. and William M. Pinson, Jr., ed., *Twenty Centuries of Great Preaching* (Waco, Tex.: Word Books, 1971), 11:198–202.

FOUR

1. Henry Sloane Coffin, *What to Preach* (New York: George H. Doran
Co., 1926), 23.

2. Andrew W. Blackwood, *Doctrinal Preaching for Today* (Grand
Rapids: Baker Book House, 1975), 189–90.

3. Cited in Roland Bartel, James S. Ackerman, and Thayer S.
Warshaw, ed., *Biblical Images in Literature* (Nashville: Abingdon
Press, 1975), 309.

4. James W. Fowler, *Stages of Faith* (New York: Harper & Row,
1981), 146–47.

5. William B. Oglesby, "Implications of Anthropology for Pastoral
Care and Counseling," *Interpretation*, 33,2 (April 1979): 163–64.

6. C. Ellis Nelson, *Where Faith Begins* (Richmond: John Knox Press,
1971), 187.

7. James White, *Introduction to Christian Worship* (Nashville:
Abingdon Press, 1980), 231.

8. John Donne, "Christmas Day, 1626" in *Sermons of John Donne,*
ed. Evelyn M. Simpson and George R. Potter (Berkeley and Los
Angeles: University of California Press, 1962), 7:279.

9. James Stewart, *A Faith to Proclaim* (New York: Charles Scribner's
Sons, 1953), 80.

10. David G. Buttrick, "Preaching on the Resurrection," *Religion in
Life,* 45,3 (Autumn 1976): 279.

11. John Killinger, "He Is Not Here," in *The Miracle of Easter,* ed.
Floyd Thatcher (Waco, Tex.: Word Books, 1980), 145.

12. Joseph A. Fitzmyer, *A Christological Catechism: New Testament*

Answers (Ramsey, N.J.: Paulist Press, 1981), 73–74.

13. Ibid., 77–79.

14. Merrill R. Abbey, *Living Doctrine in a Vital Pulpit* (Nashville: Abingdon Press, 1964), 170ff.

15. See Buttrick, *Preaching on the Resurrection*, 280–82 and Abbey, *Living Doctrine*, 167–69, 179–84.

16. Eric Baker, *Preaching Theology* (London: Epworth Press, 1954), 39–42.

17. Donald M. Baillie, *Theology of the Sacraments* (New York: Charles Scribner's Sons, 1957), 148–49.

18. Ibid., 149–50.

19. Edmund Steimle, Morris J. Niedenthal and Charles Rice, *Preaching the Story* (Philadelphia: Fortress Press, 1980).

20. Jürgen Moltmann, "He Descended into Hell . . ." in *A New Look at the Apostles' Creed*, ed. Gerhard Rein (Minneapolis: Augsburg Publishing House, 1969), 43.

21. For a program in doctrinal preaching that addresses questions 1–11 in the Heidelberg Catechism, see Heinrich Ott, *Theology and Preaching*, trans. Harold Knight (Philadelphia: Westminster Press, 1961).

22. *Sermons*, vol. 51 of *Luther's Works* (St. Louis: Concordia Publishing House; Philadelphia: Fortress Press, 1959), 135.

23. Clyde E. Fant, *Bonhoeffer: Worldly Preaching* (Nashville: Thomas Nelson and Sons, 1975), 161–65.

24. Philip Schaff, ed., *The City of God; Christian Doctrine*, vol. 2 of *The Nicene and Post-Nicene Fathers—Series I* (Grand Rapids: Wm. B. Eerdmans, 1977), 583.

25. Werner Elert, *Law and Gospel*, trans. Edward H. Schroeder (Philadelphia: Fortress Press, 1976), 1–6.

26. Karl Barth, "Gospel and Law," *Community, State, and Church: Three Essays*, ed. Will Herberg (Garden City, N.Y.: Doubleday Anchor Books, 1960), 71–100.

27. Elert, *Law and Gospel*, 38–43.

28. See Herman G. Stuempfle, Jr., *Preaching Law and Gospel* (Philadelphia: Fortress Press, 1978), 62–75 and Richard Lischer, *A Theology of Preaching* (Nashville: Abingdon Press, 1981), 58.

29. *Luther's Works*, 51: 137–61, 259–87.

30. Stuempfle, *Preaching Law and Gospel*, 23–25.

31. Donald G. Miller, "Preaching and the Law," *Pittsburgh Perspective*, 8,1 (March 1967): 20.

32. Paul Tillich, *The New Being* (New York: Charles Scribner's Sons, 1955), 3–14.

FIVE

1. Raymond E. Brown, Sprunt Lectures at Union Theological Seminary, Richmond, Va., January 1981.

2. James M. Gustafson, *Ethics from a Theocentric Perspective* (Chi-

cago: University of Chicago Press, 1981), 88ff. Also a position presented in Sprunt Lectures at Union Theological Seminary, Richmond, Va., February 1983.

3. Reinhold Niebuhr, *Justice and Mercy*, ed. Ursula M. Niebuhr (New York: Harper & Row, 1974), 14–22.

4. G. C. Berkouwer, *A Half Century of Theology* (Grand Rapids: Wm. B. Eerdmans, 1977), 26.

5. Clyde E. Fant, Jr., and William M. Pinson, Jr., ed., *Twenty Centuries of Great Preaching*, (Waco, Tex.: Word Books, 1971), 3:20–28.

6. Gilbert E. Doan, Jr., ed., *The Preaching of F. W. Robertson*, (Philadelphia: Fortress Press, 1964), 181–94.

7. George Arthur Buttrick, *Sermons Preached in a University Church* (Nashville: Abingdon Press, 1959).

8. Fant and Pinson, *Twenty Centuries*, 10:268–72.

9. W. E. Sangster, *The Craft of Sermon Construction* (Philadelphia: Westminster Press, 1951), 405–48.

10. Quincy Howe, Jr., trans. and ed. *Selected Sermons of St. Augustine* (New York: Holt, Rinehart and Winston, 1966), 71–110.

11. Ibid., 89–100.

12. Irving M. Copi, *Introduction to Logic* (New York: Macmillan Co., 1982), 92–137.

13. Ibid., 133.

14. Paul Scherer, lectures on doctrinal preaching (Union Theological Seminary, Richmond, Va., August 1956).

15. David H. C. Read, *Overheard* (Nashville: Abingdon Press, 1971). See also Robert J. McCracken, *Questions People Ask* (New York: Harper & Brothers, 1951). For an examination of the kinds of questions and problems raised in literature, compare Charles L. Rice, *Interpretation and Imagination* (Philadelphia: Fortress Press, 1970).

16. C. W. Christian, *Friedrich Schleiermacher* (Waco, Tex.: Word Books, 1979), 46.

17. Edward P. J. Corbett, *Classical Rhetoric for the Modern Student* (New York and London: Oxford University Press, 1971), 36.

18. Read, *Overheard*, 11–19.

19. David H. C. Read, *Unfinished Easter: Sermons on the Ministry* (New York: Harper & Row, 1978), 1–7.

20. See Charles F. Kemp, *Life-Situation Preaching* (St. Louis: Bethany Press, 1956); Halford E. Luccock, *In the Minister's Workshop* (Nashville: Abingdon Press, 1934), chap. 6; Robert J. McCracken, *The Making of the Sermon* (New York: Harper & Brothers, 1956), 62ff.

21. See Lionel Crocker, ed., *Harry Emerson Fosdick's Art of Preaching: An Anthology* (Springfield, Ill.: Charles C. Thomas Publisher, 1971); David G. Buttrick, "On Preaching a Parable: The Problem of Homiletic Method," *Reformed Liturgy and Music*, 17,1 (Winter 1983): 18.

22. See Wayne E. Oates, *The Christian Pastor* (Philadelphia: Westminster Press, 1977), 118–20; Ernest Edward Hunt, *Sermon Struggles* (New York: Seabury Press, 1982), 70–92. John R. Claypool's preaching and writings have also taken a turn in this more therapeutic direction. See his Lyman Beecher Lectures at Yale University and two books he authored: *The Preaching Event* (Waco, Tex.: Word Books, 1980) and *Tracks of a Fellow Struggler* (Waco, Tex.: Word Books, 1976).

23. Edgar N. Jackson, *How to Preach to People's Needs* (Grand Rapids: Baker Book House, 1972); Edmund Holt Linn, *Preaching as Counseling* (Valley Forge, Pa.: Judson Press, 1966).

24. Reuel Howe, *Partners in Preaching* (New York: Seabury Press, 1967).

25. Crocker, *Fosdick's Art of Preaching*, 13.

26. Andrew W. Blackwood, *Doctrinal Preaching for Today* (Grand Rapids: Baker Book House, 1975), 65.

27. Robert W. Duke, *The Sermon as God's Word* (Nashville: Abingdon Press, 1980), 48–63.

28. See Chrysostom's "Excessive Grief at the Death of Friends" in Fant and Pinson, *Twenty Centuries*, 1: 70–79.

29. Crocker, *Fosdick's Art of Preaching*, 246–54.

30. Philip Rieff, *Freud: The Mind of the Moralist*, rev. ed. (New York: Harper & Row, 1961), 361–93.

31. Philip Rieff, *The Triumph of the Therapeutic* (New York: Harper & Row, 1966), 26.

32. Professors of pastoral care who do not separate theology and counseling include, among others, the following: William V. Arnold, *Introduction to Pastoral Care* (Philadelphia: Westminster Press, 1982); Don S. Browning, *The Moral Context of Pastoral Care* (Philadelphia: Westminster Press, 1976); Alastair Campbell, *Rediscovering Pastoral Care* (Philadelphia: Westminster Press, 1981); Seward Hiltner, *Theological Dynamics* (Nashville: Abingdon Press, 1972); William Hulme, *Pastoral Care and Counseling* (Minneapolis: Augsburg Publishing House, 1981); Wayne E. Oates, *The Christian Pastor* (Philadelphia: Westminster Press, 1982); and William B. Oglesby, Jr., *Biblical Themes in Pastoral Care* (Nashville: Abingdon Press, 1980).

33. Donald Capps, *Pastoral Counseling and Preaching* (Philadelphia: Westminster Press, 1980), 18.

34. Ibid., 37.

35. Ibid., 41–61.

36. William V. Arnold, lecture on divorce/remarriage (Union Theological Seminary, Richmond, Va., December 1982.)

37. Capps, *Counseling and Preaching*, 98–100.

38. Ibid., 100.

39. *Luther's Works*, 51:291–99.

40. William Sloane Coffin, Jr., letter to author, 8 February 1977.

41. David O. Moberg, *The Great Reversal: Evangelism Versus Social Concern* (Philadelphia and New York: J. B. Lippincott Co., 1972).

42. Richard Mouw, *Political Evangelism* (Grand Rapids: Wm. B. Eerdmans, 1973).

43. Richard Quebedeaux, *The Young Evangelicals* (New York: Harper & Row, 1974).

44. Harold A. Bosley, *Preaching on Controversial Issues* (New York: Harper & Brothers, 1953), 115.

45. John R. W. Stott, *Between Two Worlds: The Art of Preaching in the Twentieth Century* (Grand Rapids: Wm. B. Eerdmans, 1982), 169.

46. Ibid., 159–68.

47. William Sloane Coffin, Jr., "Evangelism as Social Prophecy" (Atlanta: Forum House, 1973).

48. William Sloane Coffin, Jr., "Preaching in the Eighties" in Lyman Beecher Lectures (Yale University Visual Education Service, 1980).

49. Michael P. Hamilton, ed., *The Vietnam War: Christian Perspectives* (Grand Rapids: Wm. B. Eerdmans, 1967), 63–71.

50. Ronald J. Sider and Darrel J. Brubaker, ed., *Preaching on Peace* (Philadelphia: Fortress Press, 1982), 34–38.

51. Bruce C. Birch and Larry L. Rasmussen, *Bible and Ethics in the Christian Life* (Minneapolis: Augsburg Publishing House, 1976), 47–54, 67–71.

52. Ibid., 156–57.

53. Ibid., 152.

54. Henry Sloane Coffin, *What to Preach* (New York: George H. Doran Co., 1926), 115.

55. H. Richard Niebuhr, *Christ and Culture* (New York: Harper & Row), 29–39.

56. Ideas presented by Douglas F. Ottati in a lecture on *Christ and Culture* (Union Theological Seminary, Richmond, Va., May 1981.)

57. Carl E. Braaten, *Stewards of the Mysteries* (Minneapolis: Augsburg Publishing House, 1983), 11.

58. Josef L. Hromadka, *Impact of History on Theology* (Notre Dame: Fides Publishing, Inc., 1970), 54.

59. Carl E. Braaten, *The Future of God* (New York: Harper & Row, 1969).

60. Ibid., 147–48.

61. Eberhard Bethge, *Dietrich Bonhoeffer* (New York: Harper & Row; London: William Collins Sons, 1970), 525–26.

62. See especially Gladys Weigner and Bernhard Moosbrugger, *A Voice of the Third World: Dom Helder Camara*, trans. John Miles (Ramsey N.J.: Paulist Press, 1972).

63. Joseph Donders, *Jesus, Heaven on Earth* (Maryknoll, N.Y.: Orbis Books, 1980), 254.

64. Edmund A. Steimle, *Are You Looking for God?* (Philadelphia: Muhlenberg Press, 1957).

65. Justo L. Gonzalez and Catherine Gunsalus Gonzalez, *Liberation Preaching: The Pulpit and the Oppressed* (Nashville: Abingdon Press, 1980), 100–101; see also the Gonzalezes' sermon/Bible study presentation on this passage at a San Antonio meeting on "Creation and Justice" for the National Council of Churches of Christ in the United States in 1978.

66. Karl Rahner, *Biblical Homilies,* trans. Desmond Forristal and Richard Strachan (New York: Herder & Herder, 1966), 22–25.

67. David H. C. Read, *Religion Without Wrappings* (Grand Rapids: Wm. B. Eerdmans, 1970), 128–36.

68. Ibid., 131.

69. Emil Brunner, *The Christian Doctrine of God,* trans. Olive Wyon (Philadelphia: Westminster Press, 1950), 102.

70. Ibid.